Calm Christmas: A Simple Holiday Guide to Mindful Gift Giving, Wellness, and Traditions

Transform Your Holiday Season with Mindful Ideas, Stress-Free Celebrations, and Heartfelt Traditions for a Joyful Christmas

Clara Joy Morris

Copyright © 2024 by Clara J Morgan

All rights reserved.

No part of this book may be reproduced in any form or by any electronic or mechanical means, including information storage and retrieval systems, without written permission from the author, except for the use of brief quotations in a book review.

Contents

Review Quotes	v
INTRODUCTION: WHY A MINDFUL CHRISTMAS?	vii
1. UNDERSTANDING HOLIDAY STRESS	1
The Pressures of the Season	2
Recognizing Stress Triggers	7
Reframing Holiday Expectations	12
2. PREPARING FOR A MINDFUL HOLIDAY	19
Why Set Intentions?	20
Creating a Mindfulness Practice	24
Mindful Planning	30
3. MINDFUL GIFT-GIVING	37
Rethinking Gift Culture	38
The Joy of Thoughtful Giving	39
DIY and Experience-Based Gifts	40
4. FINDING PEACE AMID HOLIDAY CHAOS	44
Dealing with Difficult Family Dynamics	45
Mindful Communication	51
Creating Space for Yourself	57
5. MINDFUL EATING DURING THE HOLIDAYS	65
The Essence of Mindful Eating	66
Gratitude for Nourishment	69
Balancing Holiday Indulgence with Wellness	74
6. MINDFUL HOLIDAY TRADITIONS	80
Creating New, Meaningful Traditions	81
Incorporating Mindfulness into Old Traditions	85
Making Time for Reflection	91

7. STAYING PRESENT AMID THE HUSTLE	97
Mindful Moments Throughout the Day	98
Breathing Techniques for Instant Calm	99
The Power of Gratitude and Presence	101
8. MINDFUL DECORATIONS AND AMBIENCE	104
Creating a Calming Holiday Space	105
The Role of Sensory Mindfulness	106
Mindfully Simplifying the Holiday Environment	108
9. GIVING YOURSELF THE GIFT OF REST	111
Prioritizing Rest in a Busy Season	112
Creating a Restorative Holiday Routine	117
Mindful Sleep Practices	118
10. CLOSING THE YEAR WITH MINDFULNESS	123
Reflecting on the Year Past	124
Mindful Goal-Setting for the New Year	126
Conclusion: A Mindful Christmas, A Meaningful Life	135
Bonus: 30-Day Mindful Holiday Challenge	143
About the Author	151

Review Quotes

"This book transformed my holiday stress into calm joy. With each chapter, I felt more prepared to make this Christmas my most mindful yet. Highly recommended!"
— James T., Wellness Coach

"I've never felt so ready for the holidays! The advice on mindful gift-giving and simple traditions has made me actually look forward to the season instead of dreading it."

— *Sarah M., Busy Mom of Three*

"Clara's insights into self-care and setting boundaries during the holidays were a game-changer for me. Every page felt like a gift."

— *Mike L., Small Business Owner*

"This is the holiday guide I didn't know I needed. Beautifully written, easy to follow, and full of heartfelt wisdom. My family noticed the difference in me, and I enjoyed every moment."

— *Tina W., Mindfulness Enthusiast*

"Forget the usual holiday rush—this book is all about savoring the season. I finally feel ready to have a calm Christmas!"

— *Olivia P., School Teacher*

INTRODUCTION: WHY A MINDFUL CHRISTMAS?

The holiday season is often painted as a time of joy, connection, and warmth. It's portrayed in commercials as a world of glowing lights, laughter around the table, and perfectly wrapped gifts under the tree. Yet, for many of us, the reality of the holidays looks different. It can be a whirlwind of stress, unmet expectations, and an unending to-do list that leaves us more exhausted than uplifted. Between family gatherings, gift shopping, decorating, and a steady stream of holiday obligations, it's easy to feel like we're racing toward the finish line rather than savoring each moment.

Setting the Tone for the Holidays

The holidays have a unique way of amplifying stress. We feel pressure to create memorable experiences, cook perfect meals, and show up for every social gathering — all while managing our usual responsibilities. Social media adds another layer to this as we're constantly exposed to idealized images of other people's celebrations, which can make us question whether we're doing enough or doing it "right."

Yet, behind the scenes, many are silently juggling personal challenges. There are those dealing with grief, struggling financially, or facing difficult family dynamics. Even for those not dealing with overt challenges, the pressure to meet societal and personal expectations can be overwhelming. We find ourselves worrying about giving the right gifts, planning the right events, and making everything "perfect," only to feel hollow and exhausted by the time New Year's arrives.

The Toll of Holiday Stress

The toll of holiday stress is more than emotional; it's physical, too. The impact of stress on our bodies during this season can lead to disrupted sleep, digestive issues, headaches, and a weakened immune system. Studies have shown that heightened stress weakens our body's ability to fend off illness, which might explain why many of us get sick right around the holidays. Mentally, stress clouds our ability to focus and enjoy the present moment, making it difficult to truly appreciate the gatherings, the meals, and the time spent with loved ones.

When we're constantly thinking about what's next on our holiday agenda or comparing our celebrations to idealized images, we're robbing ourselves of the opportunity to enjoy what we have right in front of us. This tendency to be in a perpetual state of planning or comparing can lead to feelings of anxiety, sadness, and even resentment. Ironically, in our quest to create a picture-perfect holiday, we lose the very joy and warmth we're aiming for.

Why a Mindful Approach?

Mindfulness is about more than just staying calm; it's about fully engaging with the present moment and embracing it without judgment. By taking a mindful approach to the holidays, we give ourselves permission to slow down, breathe, and savor each experience. It's a chance to break free from the cycle of stress and enter a space where we can genuinely feel grateful, content, and present.

Choosing mindfulness for the holiday season isn't about renouncing traditions or giving up on holiday fun; instead, it's about letting go of the unnecessary pressure and focusing on what truly matters. A mindful Christmas is about shifting our perspective from achieving perfection to fostering connection, gratitude, and joy. It's about deciding that the quality of our presence is more valuable than the quantity of presents or the extravagance of our celebrations.

Mindfulness invites us to embrace the holidays as they are — to appreciate both the beauty and the imperfections. When we adopt this approach, we're more likely to enjoy the little moments, from the scent of cinnamon in the kitchen to the warmth of a shared laugh with friends. We're also better equipped to handle the inevitable challenges, from awkward family conversations to last-minute schedule changes. With mindfulness, these experiences no longer feel like obstacles to an ideal holiday but part of the tapestry of a real, meaningful celebration.

What is Mindfulness?

In a world where we're often encouraged to do more, be more, and achieve more, the concept of mindfulness offers a refreshing pause. At its core, mindfulness is a practice of fully experiencing the present moment with a sense of curiosity and without judgment. It's about being where you are, feeling what you're feeling, and letting go of the constant need to control, perfect, or predict what comes next.

Mindfulness isn't new; it has roots in ancient spiritual traditions, especially within Buddhism. However, over the past few decades, mindfulness has been widely embraced across cultures and settings. From schools to workplaces and therapy rooms, the practice has been shown to improve mental health, reduce stress, and enhance well-being. So, why not apply it to our busiest, most demanding season of the year — the holiday season?

During the holidays, mindfulness can become our secret ingredient for turning a hectic schedule into an opportunity for calm and presence. It can help us handle holiday stressors, respond thoughtfully in challenging situations, and cultivate a sense of joy that goes beyond the surface. Let's take a closer look at what mindfulness means, how it works, and how it can be uniquely applied to make our holidays truly meaningful.

What Exactly is Mindfulness?

Mindfulness is often described as paying attention, on purpose, to the present moment, without judgment. It sounds simple, but it's surprisingly challenging to maintain in our daily lives, especially in a season full of distractions. Imagine sitting down for a family dinner but instead of fully engaging in the conversation, your mind is wandering — thinking about tomorrow's to-do list, stressing about a gift that hasn't arrived, or wondering if everyone is enjoying themselves. When we're in this state, we're physically present but mentally elsewhere, missing out on the moments that make the holidays special.

By practicing mindfulness, we can learn to redirect our attention back to the present moment whenever we catch ourselves drifting. It's a gentle way of reminding ourselves that this moment, however imperfect, is worth noticing. Mindfulness allows us to step out of autopilot mode and experience each event, each interaction, each breath more fully.

The Benefits of Mindfulness

The benefits of mindfulness are backed by science, with numerous studies confirming its positive impact on both mental and physical health. Here are some key benefits that can make a difference during the holiday season:

- **Reduced Stress**: Mindfulness has been shown to reduce levels of cortisol, the body's stress hormone. This is crucial during the holidays, when stress can reach its peak due to endless tasks, financial worries, and social obligations.
- **Improved Emotional Regulation**: Mindfulness helps us respond to situations rather than react impulsively. When we're mindful, we're better able to handle emotional triggers like tense family dynamics or holiday disappointments with grace and patience.
- **Enhanced Focus and Presence**: Being mindful allows us to focus on one task at a time, which can lead to more enjoyable and less overwhelming experiences. Instead of juggling five holiday tasks simultaneously, we can focus on decorating, cooking, or wrapping gifts one at a time, savoring the act itself.
- **Greater Joy and Gratitude**: Mindfulness encourages us to notice and appreciate the small things, such as the warmth of a cup of tea, the sound of laughter, or the soft glow of holiday lights. These tiny

moments can bring immense joy and gratitude when we take the time to notice them.

Applying Mindfulness to the Holidays

So how can we bring this practice of mindfulness into a season known for its busyness? It starts with intention and small, manageable shifts in our approach.

1. **Set Intentions Rather Than Expectations**: Rather than striving to create a "perfect" holiday, set an intention to experience the holiday season fully. Intentions are flexible, while expectations are rigid and often lead to disappointment. For example, you might set an intention to "be present with family" rather than expecting a flawless family gathering.
2. **Slow Down and Savor Moments**: When decorating, baking, or even wrapping presents, give yourself permission to slow down. Notice the scents, textures, and colors around you. If you're wrapping a gift, feel the texture of the paper, hear the snip of the scissors, and see the colors you've chosen. This makes each task feel more enjoyable and less like a chore.
3. **Practice Gratitude**: During the holidays, gratitude is often focused on material things — gifts, decorations, or fancy meals. Try to shift the focus by practicing gratitude for the people you're with, the time you have together, or even simple comforts like a cozy blanket or a warm drink. Gratitude helps shift our perspective from what's missing to what's already here.
4. **Take Breaks to Breathe**: It's easy to go non-stop during the holidays, but taking a few moments to pause and breathe can make all the difference. When

you feel overwhelmed, take a few slow, deep breaths. This small act helps ground you, calming both body and mind so that you're better able to handle the next task or conversation.
5. **Mindful Listening**: When you're with family and friends, practice listening mindfully. This means putting aside thoughts of what you'll say next and simply being present with what the other person is saying. Mindful listening can lead to more meaningful conversations and connections, creating memories that are richer and more fulfilling.

Embracing the Imperfections

Mindfulness also teaches us the art of embracing imperfections. The holiday season rarely goes exactly as planned. There may be moments of frustration, unexpected events, or even disappointments. Mindfulness encourages us to accept these imperfections with grace, to see them as part of the experience rather than obstacles to an ideal holiday.

When we let go of the need for perfection, we open ourselves to a more honest, meaningful holiday season. We're able to laugh off small mishaps, roll with last-minute changes, and appreciate the beauty of things as they are. The practice of mindfulness isn't about making everything go smoothly; it's about staying present and finding peace amid the holiday's ups and downs.

The Purpose of This Book

The holiday season holds a special place in our lives. It's a time when we seek connection, cherish traditions, and often pause to reflect on the year gone by. Yet, as we've seen, it's also a season that can bring about stress, overwhelm, and a feeling of being caught up in a whirlwind of expectations. This book is here to offer a new approach to the holiday season: one rooted in mindfulness, presence, and joy.

A mindful approach to the holidays isn't about retreating from the festivities or discarding beloved traditions. Instead, it's about transforming how we engage with the season. It's about finding ways to be more present with loved ones, reducing the mental and emotional strain, and discovering moments of joy and peace amid the busyness. Throughout this book, you'll find practical strategies and gentle reminders designed to help you experience the holidays in a more meaningful, grounded way.

Setting Realistic Expectations

This book isn't a guide to creating a perfect holiday. In fact, it's quite the opposite. Here, we focus on embracing the imperfections, the unexpected twists, and the little moments that make each holiday season unique. You won't find pressure to host an elaborate dinner party, nor will you feel compelled to achieve a picture-perfect aesthetic. Instead, the pages ahead offer realistic, practical guidance on how to reduce stress and cultivate calm, regardless of how or where you choose to celebrate.

For some, a mindful holiday may look like simplifying gift-giving. For others, it might mean setting boundaries around social events, or creating time for personal reflection amid the gatherings. Whatever your situation, this book is here to meet you where you are and offer a toolkit for navigating the season with presence and purpose.

What You'll Gain

Here's what you can expect to take away from this journey into a mindful holiday season:

1. **Practical Mindfulness Techniques**: From simple breathing exercises to grounding practices, you'll learn techniques to help you stay calm and present, even when the season feels overwhelming. These exercises are designed to be quick and accessible, so you can weave them into your routine without adding to your holiday load.
2. **Stress-Reduction Strategies**: The holidays bring unique stressors, from financial pressures to social dynamics. This book offers practical ways to manage these stressors, helping you set boundaries, prioritize self-care, and keep your focus on what truly matters to you. You'll find specific techniques for handling common holiday stressors, from managing finances to navigating family gatherings.
3. **Mindful Communication and Connection**: Mindfulness isn't just about personal practices; it's also about how we interact with others. Here, you'll discover ways to bring mindfulness into your relationships during the holidays, fostering more meaningful connections and reducing friction. Whether it's through mindful listening, setting compassionate boundaries, or being present with loved ones, you'll learn ways to make each interaction more intentional.
4. **Gift-Giving with Heart**: In a season often focused on material gifts, we'll explore how to give gifts in a mindful way. You'll learn to choose gifts that truly resonate with the recipient, bringing thoughtfulness and authenticity back to the process. Beyond the physical items, we'll also discuss the art of giving intangible gifts — like time, kindness, and shared experiences.

5. **Creating New, Mindful Traditions**: Many of us follow traditions that don't fully resonate or bring joy. This book invites you to explore what traditions feel meaningful to you and encourages you to create new rituals that align with your values. Whether it's starting a gratitude practice, planning a quiet day for self-care, or volunteering, you'll find inspiration for making the season your own.
6. **Embracing Gratitude and Joy**: Mindfulness teaches us that joy isn't always in grand gestures but in the small, everyday moments. This book encourages you to slow down and notice these moments — the scent of a holiday candle, the warmth of a cozy blanket, or a moment of laughter with a friend. Through gratitude practices and reflection prompts, you'll cultivate a deeper sense of appreciation for the season's simple pleasures.

How to Use This Book

Each chapter in this book focuses on a different aspect of the holiday season, from gift-giving to gathering with family and friends. At the end of each chapter, you'll find practical exercises, reflection prompts, and mindful practices to help you put the concepts into action. Feel free to move through the book at your own pace, choosing the chapters that resonate most or applying practices as needed. There is no right or wrong way to read this book — it's here to support you on your journey toward a more mindful holiday.

This book also recognizes that everyone's holiday experience is different. You may be celebrating with family, with friends, with a partner, or on your own. You may have religious traditions or secular ones, and you may celebrate different holidays altogether. The practices in this book are meant to be adaptable, so you can shape them to fit your own unique holiday experience.

A Note on Self-Compassion

As you move through the chapters, remember to bring a sense of self-compassion to your journey. The goal here isn't to be "perfectly mindful" but to take small steps toward a more grounded and joyful holiday season. You may find that some practices come easily, while others feel challenging or unfamiliar. Embrace each practice with an open heart, and remember that there's no need to rush or force yourself into anything that doesn't resonate.

Sometimes, the most mindful thing we can do is let go of the pressure we place on ourselves. So, as you read, be gentle with yourself. There's no single "right" way to experience the holidays, and no expectation that you'll get it all "right." The simple act of trying to be more present, to notice the little moments, and to cultivate joy is enough.

Moving Forward

The purpose of this book is to help you approach the holiday season with a mindset of peace, presence, and joy. It's an invitation to pause, to breathe, and to create a holiday that feels truly meaningful. By practicing mindfulness, we can let go of the need for perfection and instead focus on what truly matters — connection, gratitude, and the beauty of the present moment.

So, as you begin this journey, take a moment to set an intention. Ask yourself what you most hope to gain from a mindful holiday season. Perhaps it's a greater sense of calm, a deeper connection with loved ones, or simply a holiday where you feel like yourself. Let this intention guide you, and let the practices within these pages support you along the way.

In the chapters ahead, we'll dive into each aspect of the holiday season, exploring practical strategies to bring mindfulness into your celebrations. From learning how to handle holiday stress to creating new, meaningful traditions, you'll find tools to help you craft a holiday experience that brings you genuine joy.

Together, let's create a holiday season that reflects what truly matters to you — one filled with presence, peace, and a sense of mindful celebration.

Chapter 1
Understanding Holiday Stress

For many of us, the holidays are a time of mixed emotions. We look forward to the warmth, connection, and joy, but we're also acutely aware of the stress, pressure, and obligations that come along with it. This chapter dives into the sources of holiday stress and helps illuminate why the season can feel overwhelming — even when we want to enjoy it.

The pressures of the holiday season stem from a variety of expectations, both internal and external. These expectations shape how we approach the holidays, often causing us to place ourselves under tremendous stress. By understanding these sources, we can begin to identify what's driving our stress and take steps to reduce it.

The Pressures of the Season

The holiday season carries a unique set of pressures that can make even the most joyful aspects feel like burdens. Below are some of the most common sources of holiday stress and how they tend to manifest.

1. **Family Expectations**: For many, family is central to holiday celebrations, and time spent with loved ones can be both fulfilling and stressful. Family expectations can create pressure to attend gatherings, maintain traditions, or even manage difficult family dynamics. For some, being around family stirs up old conflicts or creates tension. For others, the obligation to host or attend large family gatherings feels daunting. Family expectations often stem from a desire for connection but can easily turn into stress when they feel forced or obligatory.
2. **Financial Burdens**: The holidays are often accompanied by financial strain, as we feel the need to purchase gifts, decorate, travel, and host events. For some, this pressure can overshadow the joy of giving or celebrating. Financial worries can lead to guilt, anxiety, and a sense of inadequacy when we feel we can't "measure up" to societal or personal standards. This pressure is compounded by commercial messages that tell us our love or appreciation is tied to what we buy, rather than the moments we share.

3. **Social Obligations**: During the holidays, social gatherings multiply, whether they're with friends, family, or coworkers. Many of us feel obligated to attend events out of a sense of duty rather than desire. For introverts, this can lead to social burnout, while for others, it can create pressure to meet social expectations around holiday spirit, cheerfulness, and togetherness. Attending social events when we don't truly feel connected to them can leave us feeling drained rather than uplifted.
4. **Traditions and the Pressure to "Do It All"**: Holiday traditions are beautiful, but they can also feel burdensome if they become rigid or if we try to do too much. When we feel the need to uphold every tradition, decorate perfectly, or cook every special dish, the joy of the holiday can quickly turn into an exhausting checklist. Traditions can become especially challenging when they no longer align with our values or life circumstances but we feel pressured to keep them going for the sake of others.
5. **Self-Expectations**: Sometimes the pressure comes from within. We set high expectations for how we want the holidays to look, how we want to feel, and how we want others to feel. This can lead to a perfectionist mindset, where we're constantly striving to make everything just right, from the decorations to the meal planning. Self-expectations can be particularly tough because they're rooted in our desire to make the holidays meaningful, yet they often lead us to feel inadequate if things don't turn out as planned.

Recognizing Stress Triggers

The first step in managing holiday stress is learning to recognize what specifically triggers it for you. Everyone's experience is unique, and while some people may be triggered by financial worries, others might feel stress from family dynamics or a packed social calendar. By identifying these triggers, you can take steps to mitigate them and approach the season with greater awareness and compassion.

Here are some practical ways to identify your holiday stress triggers:

1. **Observe Your Reactions**: Take note of moments when you feel overwhelmed, anxious, or frustrated. Are these feelings linked to certain people, events, or tasks? Observing your emotional reactions can help you identify the source of your stress and consider ways to manage it.
2. **Keep a Holiday Journal**: Jot down your feelings about the holiday season in a journal, noting what activities or interactions bring you joy versus what feels burdensome. Patterns will start to emerge, showing you which parts of the holiday are nourishing and which are draining.
3. **Ask Yourself "Why?"**: When you feel stressed about a particular aspect of the holidays, ask yourself why it's causing tension. For example, if buying gifts is a source of stress, is it because of financial pressure, time constraints, or uncertainty about what others will appreciate? Understanding the "why" can help you find solutions that directly address the root cause of your stress.
4. **Notice Physical Symptoms**: Sometimes stress manifests physically before we're even consciously

aware of it. Pay attention to signs of stress in your body, such as headaches, muscle tension, or digestive issues. These physical cues can be signals that something about your holiday routine is creating stress.
5. **Consider Your Inner Dialogue**: Reflect on any internal pressure you're placing on yourself to meet certain standards. Are you stressing over creating a perfect holiday? Feeling anxious about meeting family expectations? This inner dialogue can be an important source of insight, helping you become aware of self-imposed pressures that may not be necessary.

Reframing Holiday Expectations

Once you've recognized your triggers, the next step is to reframe your expectations and approach the holidays with a mindset that reduces stress rather than increases it. Here are some strategies to help you set realistic expectations and focus on what truly matters to you.

1. **Define What Matters Most**: Take a moment to reflect on what makes the holidays meaningful to you. Is it spending time with family? Relaxing and recharging? Giving back to the community? By defining what matters most, you can prioritize those aspects and let go of tasks that don't align with your values.
2. **Embrace Flexibility**: Life changes, and so do our circumstances. Traditions or expectations that made sense in the past might not fit our current lives. Allow yourself the flexibility to adapt your holiday plans based on what feels achievable and fulfilling now,

rather than forcing yourself to uphold every past tradition.
3. **Set Boundaries**: Boundaries are crucial during the holidays. Whether it's financial, emotional, or social boundaries, it's okay to say no to certain obligations or ask for support when you need it. Setting limits on spending, limiting the number of social events, or even setting boundaries with family members can help you manage your stress and protect your well-being.
4. **Practice Self-Compassion**: If things don't go as planned, practice self-compassion. The holidays can be unpredictable, and it's natural to experience some stress or disappointment. By treating yourself with kindness and accepting that not everything has to be perfect, you can navigate the season with a lighter heart and a greater sense of peace.
5. **Set Intentions Rather Than Goals**: Instead of setting rigid goals for how you want the holiday to unfold, set intentions. For example, rather than aiming for a perfect holiday meal, set an intention to enjoy the time with loved ones, regardless of how the meal turns out. Intentions are about the quality of the experience rather than the outcome, which can help you feel more fulfilled even if things aren't picture-perfect.
6. **Embrace Minimalism in Celebration**: Scaling back doesn't mean sacrificing joy. Sometimes, less is more. Consider focusing on a few meaningful activities or gatherings rather than spreading yourself thin with countless events. Minimalism in holiday celebration isn't about having "less" but about enjoying "more" of what genuinely matters.

Recognizing Stress Triggers

In our journey to create a mindful holiday season, one of the most essential steps is identifying the unique stress triggers that affect each of us. While the previous chapter explored the common pressures of the holiday season, this chapter focuses on the personal, specific elements that cause each of us to feel overwhelmed. Recognizing these individual stress triggers allows us to avoid spiraling into seasonal stress and provides us with the insight needed to approach the holidays with greater awareness and resilience.

Everyone has different triggers. For one person, it might be financial strain; for another, it could be the tension of family gatherings or the loneliness that can arise during the holidays. Identifying these triggers isn't about labeling holiday experiences as "good" or "bad" but rather understanding where our personal stress points lie so that we can navigate the season with greater ease.

The Importance of Recognizing Personal Triggers

When we're unaware of our triggers, we're more susceptible to reacting to them impulsively. For instance, if holiday shopping is a financial trigger, we might procrastinate or overspend in an attempt to ease the tension. If family gatherings are stressful, we might withdraw or, conversely, feel compelled to go overboard trying to please everyone. Recognizing triggers gives us a choice in how we respond, allowing us to meet these situations with more intentionality and less emotional reactivity.

By identifying what specifically triggers stress for us, we can create a holiday experience that better honors our mental and emotional well-being. This awareness also empowers us to communicate our needs, set boundaries, and make mindful choices that reflect what matters most.

How to Identify Your Holiday Stress Triggers

Identifying personal triggers requires a combination of self-reflection, observation, and honest evaluation. Below are several exercises to help you explore the underlying causes of your holiday stress.

1. **Reflect on Past Experiences**: Think back to previous holiday seasons and consider what moments, people, or situations caused you to feel overwhelmed or anxious. Perhaps a family gathering led to conflict, or an ambitious cooking project left you exhausted. Writing down these memories can help you pinpoint patterns in your holiday experiences.
2. **Notice Your Physical Reactions**: Our bodies often give us signals of stress before we're consciously aware of it. Pay attention to physical signs like tension in the shoulders, shallow breathing, or an upset stomach. If you notice these reactions at certain times — perhaps while shopping, preparing for a gathering, or planning holiday events — they can provide clues to your triggers.
3. **Monitor Your Emotions**: Take note of moments when you feel heightened emotions such as anxiety, irritability, sadness, or frustration. Emotional reactions often reveal deeper stress points, especially if they arise repeatedly in similar contexts. For instance, if you feel resentful about hosting responsibilities, the underlying trigger may be the pressure of handling everything on your own.

4. **Identify Self-Imposed Pressures**: Sometimes, the most intense stress comes from expectations we set for ourselves. Reflect on any inner pressure you feel to create a "perfect" holiday, whether it's about decorating, gift-giving, or fulfilling traditions. Recognizing these self-imposed pressures can help you decide which expectations are truly meaningful and which can be adjusted.
5. **List Potential Stressful Situations**: Make a list of specific holiday activities or interactions you anticipate and rate how each one makes you feel on a scale from 1 (no stress) to 10 (extreme stress). This exercise can help you predict and prepare for potential stressors by allowing you to mentally and emotionally prepare in advance.

Common Holiday Stress Triggers

While each person's experience is unique, there are some common holiday triggers that many people encounter. Below are a few examples to consider as you reflect on your own potential triggers:

- **Financial Concerns**: Shopping, gift-giving, travel, and hosting can all put pressure on our finances. If financial stress is a trigger, consider setting a realistic budget before the season begins and sticking to it, or explore alternative ways to show appreciation that don't involve spending beyond your means.
- **Family Dynamics**: Family gatherings can stir up old conflicts, amplify family tensions, or bring out unresolved issues. If family dynamics are a stressor, try setting boundaries with family members or limiting the time you spend at gatherings that feel challenging.

- **Overcommitment**: Saying yes to every invitation and obligation can quickly lead to burnout. If overcommitment is a trigger, practice saying "no" with kindness and prioritize the gatherings that genuinely bring you joy and connection.
- **Travel Stress**: Navigating airports, traffic, or public transportation during peak holiday times can be exhausting. If travel is a trigger, plan ahead as much as possible, giving yourself time buffers to reduce last-minute anxiety. Consider virtual gatherings as an alternative if travel proves too stressful.
- **Loneliness or Isolation**: For some, the holidays can magnify feelings of loneliness, especially if they're far from family or have experienced loss. If loneliness is a trigger, consider connecting with friends or volunteering in the community, as helping others can foster a sense of connection and purpose.
- **Pressure to Maintain Traditions**: Traditions are beautiful, but they can also feel stifling if they're no longer meaningful. If the pressure to uphold traditions is a trigger, give yourself permission to create new traditions or modify existing ones to better suit your current life.

Developing Strategies to Manage Your Triggers

Once you've identified your stress triggers, you can take proactive steps to manage them. Below are a few strategies to help you address specific triggers with mindfulness and compassion.

1. **Set Boundaries in Advance**: If certain activities or gatherings are stress-inducing, establish boundaries beforehand. This might mean limiting the time you

spend at a family event, setting a spending limit for gifts, or deciding in advance how many holiday events you'll attend. Boundaries can help you avoid burnout and give you the space to enjoy the season on your own terms.

2. **Prepare a "Stress-Relief Toolkit"**: Identify simple activities or tools that help calm you down when you feel triggered. This toolkit might include deep breathing exercises, a short walk, listening to calming music, or a quick journaling session. Having these tools on hand can help you de-escalate stress before it becomes overwhelming.

3. **Plan Ahead**: Organization can ease anxiety for certain triggers, especially when it comes to holiday shopping, cooking, or travel. Make a list of things to do, prioritize tasks, and spread them out over the season so that they don't all pile up at once. Planning also allows you to feel more in control and reduces last-minute stress.

4. **Cultivate a Practice of Letting Go**: Recognize that the holidays don't have to be perfect. Practice letting go of expectations that create unnecessary pressure. If something doesn't go as planned, remind yourself that it doesn't define the success of your holiday experience. The art of letting go can be liberating and help you approach the season with a lighter heart.

5. **Communicate Your Needs**: If certain family dynamics or social obligations are a source of stress, consider discussing your needs with the people involved. Honest, respectful communication can go a long way in diffusing tension. Let others know how you're feeling and what might help you enjoy the

season more, whether it's a smaller gathering, a different tradition, or a shared responsibility.
6. **Practice Self-Compassion**: The holidays are a season of giving, and that includes giving to yourself. Treat yourself with kindness, especially when stress triggers arise. Remind yourself that it's natural to feel stress during this busy time, and practice forgiving yourself if things don't go exactly as planned.

Turning Triggers into Opportunities for Growth

Holiday stress triggers, while challenging, also present an opportunity for personal growth. Each time you become aware of a trigger, you're given a chance to deepen your understanding of your own needs and boundaries. This awareness empowers you to make choices that honor your well-being and prioritize what truly matters.

As you move forward with this mindfulness practice, keep in mind that change doesn't happen overnight. Recognizing triggers is an ongoing process, and each holiday season provides new insights. By building awareness and compassion toward yourself, you'll develop a stronger foundation for navigating the season with grace and resilience.

Reframing Holiday Expectations

Holiday expectations can be tricky. Whether they stem from societal ideals, family traditions, or our own desires to make the season memorable, expectations can often set us up for disappointment, stress, and frustration. While it's natural to want a holiday filled with joy, beauty, and connection, the pressure to create a flawless experience can cloud what the season is truly about. This chapter focuses on redefining our holiday expectations in a way that brings peace, connection, and meaning rather than stress or anxiety.

Reframing holiday expectations means aligning the season's activities and interactions with what genuinely matters to us. It's about embracing a mindset of flexibility and compassion, letting go of ideals that don't serve us, and replacing them with intentions that bring us closer to a sense of fulfillment and joy. This chapter will guide you through practical strategies to help you set realistic expectations, honor what's meaningful to you, and embrace an approach to the holidays that feels authentic.

The Impact of Unrealistic Expectations

Unrealistic expectations are one of the most common sources of holiday stress. They can cause us to overspend, overcommit, and push ourselves to the point of burnout. When we envision the "perfect" holiday — complete with ideal decorations, beautifully prepared meals, harmonious family gatherings, and thoughtfully chosen gifts — we set ourselves up for a kind of perfectionism that can be impossible to achieve. The result is often disappointment, exhaustion, and a sense that we're "falling short" or missing out.

Expectations can be especially challenging because they're often reinforced by cultural messages and social media. Advertisements depict cozy family gatherings, elaborate meals, and immaculate decorations, creating a standard that's often unrealistic. Social media adds another layer, as we see curated images of other people's holidays, which can amplify feelings of comparison and inadequacy.

By recognizing these expectations and shifting them toward what's realistic and meaningful, we can create a holiday that is genuinely fulfilling, allowing us to enjoy the season without unnecessary stress.

Setting Realistic Holiday Expectations

Reframing holiday expectations begins with recognizing the difference between ideals and reality. Here are some steps to help you set realistic expectations for a holiday that feels both manageable and meaningful.

1. **Reflect on What Matters Most**: Take time to consider what you value most about the holiday season. Is it spending time with family, creating new memories, relaxing, or giving back? By identifying the aspects that bring you joy and purpose, you can prioritize these over activities that feel obligatory or unfulfilling. Ask yourself: if you had to simplify the holiday down to a few essential elements, what would those be?
2. **Let Go of the Pressure for Perfection**: Recognize that the holidays don't need to look or feel perfect to be meaningful. Embrace a "good enough" mindset, where you allow yourself to enjoy the season without stressing over every detail. Rather than striving for flawless decorations or the perfect family photo, focus on creating moments that feel genuine and enjoyable.
3. **Set Boundaries Around Obligations**: Family and social obligations can add significant pressure during the holidays. If certain gatherings or commitments feel draining, give yourself permission to say no or set boundaries that work for you. It's okay to decline an invitation, leave a gathering early, or skip an event altogether if it helps you maintain your peace and well-being.
4. **Simplify Gift-Giving**: The expectation to give numerous or extravagant gifts can create both financial

and emotional strain. Consider simplifying your approach by focusing on gifts that are meaningful rather than costly. You might also explore alternative ways to show appreciation, such as giving experiences, creating handmade gifts, or spending quality time together. If gift exchanges feel overwhelming, talk to family members about simplifying the tradition.

5. **Practice Self-Compassion**: If things don't go as planned, remember to treat yourself with kindness and understanding. The holidays are inherently unpredictable, and even the best-laid plans can change. Instead of dwelling on what didn't go right, focus on the moments of joy that did happen. Self-compassion helps you stay grounded and reminds you that it's okay for things to be imperfect.

Strategies for Embracing a Mindful, Flexible Holiday

One of the keys to enjoying a holiday season free from rigid expectations is cultivating a mindset of mindfulness and flexibility. This allows us to adapt to changes, embrace imperfections, and focus on the present moment rather than striving for an idealized experience. Below are strategies for embracing a more mindful and flexible approach to the season.

1. **Set Intentions, Not Goals**: Instead of setting specific goals for the holidays, try setting intentions that focus on the quality of your experience rather than the outcome. For instance, rather than aiming for a "perfect" dinner, set an intention to enjoy the process of cooking and connecting with others over the meal. Intentions are adaptable, which allows you to

flow with the season rather than feeling restricted by fixed goals.

2. **Create a Holiday "Must-Have" List**: Make a list of the few essential activities or traditions that bring you joy and feel meaningful. These might include baking cookies with family, decorating the tree, or watching a favorite holiday movie. By identifying these "must-haves," you can let go of other activities that don't hold as much significance, freeing up time and energy for what truly matters.

3. **Be Present in Each Moment**: Mindfulness teaches us to appreciate the present, even when it's imperfect. During holiday gatherings or events, focus on being fully engaged with the people and activities around you. Listen actively, savor each bite of food, and allow yourself to truly experience the moment without worrying about what comes next. Being present helps you appreciate the season in a way that goes beyond external expectations.

4. **Embrace Imperfections as Part of the Season**: Remind yourself that small mishaps or unexpected changes are natural and can even add charm to your holiday memories. If the meal doesn't go as planned, the decorations aren't picture-perfect, or a gift exchange goes awry, take it in stride. These imperfections often become the stories we laugh about and remember fondly, so embrace them as part of the journey.

5. **Communicate Your Needs and Intentions**: Talk openly with family and friends about your holiday approach and any changes you'd like to make. This might include discussing alternative gift-giving ideas, setting boundaries around gatherings, or

creating new traditions. Clear communication can help set expectations and prevent misunderstandings, allowing you to celebrate in a way that aligns with your values.

Finding Joy in Simplicity

In reframing holiday expectations, one of the most profound shifts is learning to find joy in simplicity. The essence of the holidays doesn't lie in elaborate decorations, perfect gatherings, or expensive gifts, but in the moments of connection, warmth, and gratitude. When we simplify, we create space to fully experience these elements, appreciating the holiday season in its truest form.

Consider choosing one or two simple, meaningful activities that help you connect with loved ones and experience gratitude. This could be as simple as sharing a meal, going for a walk together, or reflecting on the past year over a cup of hot chocolate. These moments don't require perfection; they simply require presence.

Simplicity also applies to how we approach ourselves. Instead of striving to be the "perfect" host, family member, or friend, let yourself simply be present and authentic. By focusing on the quality of your interactions rather than the quantity of tasks you accomplish, you can cultivate a holiday experience that is both manageable and fulfilling.

Moving Forward

Reframing holiday expectations isn't about lowering your standards or giving up on the magic of the season. It's about redefining what a meaningful holiday looks like for you, based on values, authenticity, and mindfulness rather than external pressures. By focusing on what truly matters, setting realistic expectations, and embracing a mindset of flexibility, you can approach the holidays with a sense of peace and fulfillment.

In the upcoming chapters, we'll continue exploring practical ways to bring mindfulness into specific aspects of the holiday season, from gatherings with family to gift-giving and self-care. As you move forward, hold onto the idea that the holidays are not a performance to be perfected but a time to experience, savor, and enjoy in a way that feels genuine to you.

Remember, the true beauty of the season lies in the moments we share, the connections we make, and the love we give — both to others and to ourselves. By letting go of rigid expectations and embracing a holiday that reflects your values, you'll find that the season holds all the meaning you need, in its own imperfect, wonderful way.

Chapter 2
Preparing for a Mindful Holiday

This chapter will guide you through the process of setting mindful intentions for the holidays. Whether your intention is to cultivate gratitude, embrace simplicity, or foster connections, defining what matters most can help you stay focused, calm, and grounded as the season unfolds. Intentions serve as anchors, gently reminding us of our purpose and helping us avoid getting swept up in stress, expectations, or distractions.
Setting Intentions for the Season

Setting intentions is one of the most powerful ways to create a mindful holiday season. Unlike goals, which are often tied to specific outcomes, intentions focus on the quality of our experiences and the mindset we want to bring to each moment. Setting intentions is about clarifying what truly matters to us and how we want to show up, both for ourselves and for others. By taking time to define our intentions for the holidays, we can create a season that feels meaningful, joyful, and aligned with our values.

Why Set Intentions?

Intentions create a roadmap for how we want to experience the holidays. While we can't control every aspect of the season, we can choose how we respond to situations, engage with others, and care for ourselves. Setting intentions allows us to approach each day, event, and interaction with greater awareness.

For example, if your intention is to enjoy quality time with family, this can shape your choices around gatherings, gift-giving, and activities. You might prioritize events that foster closeness and let go of obligations that feel less meaningful. Intentions help us stay true to ourselves, giving the season a sense of purpose and depth beyond simply checking off holiday tasks.

Steps to Set Your Holiday Intentions

Setting intentions is a reflective process. Here's a step-by-step guide to help you identify what you want to focus on this holiday season.

1. **Reflect on Past Holidays**: Take a moment to think back on past holiday seasons. What memories bring you joy? What experiences felt stressful or unfulfilling? By reflecting on what has or hasn't

worked in the past, you can gain insight into what you'd like to create or change this year.
2. **Identify Your Core Values**: Think about your personal values and what's important to you, especially during the holidays. Is it connection, gratitude, peace, or perhaps generosity? These values will serve as the foundation for your intentions, guiding you toward experiences that align with your sense of purpose.
3. **Envision Your Ideal Holiday Season**: Close your eyes and imagine your ideal holiday season. Picture the people, activities, and emotions you want to experience. Ask yourself: how do you want to feel? What does a meaningful holiday look like to you? Use this vision to help you define the kind of holiday you'd like to create.
4. **Choose One to Three Key Intentions**: Rather than overloading yourself with too many expectations, choose one to three core intentions for the season. These should be simple, clear, and aligned with your values. For example, you might choose intentions like "cultivate calm," "foster connection," or "embrace gratitude." Having a few focused intentions helps keep your priorities clear and manageable.
5. **Write Down Your Intentions**: Writing down your intentions solidifies them and serves as a tangible reminder throughout the season. Place them somewhere visible, like on your fridge, your journal, or a sticky note on your mirror. Whenever you feel stressed or overwhelmed, revisit your intentions to realign and refocus.

Examples of Holiday Intentions

Below are some examples of holiday intentions to inspire your own. Feel free to personalize these or create entirely new ones that resonate with your unique vision for the season.

- **Prioritize Connection**: "I intend to spend quality time with loved ones and focus on creating meaningful moments together."
- **Embrace Gratitude**: "I intend to approach each day with gratitude, finding joy in the small moments and appreciating what I have."
- **Cultivate Calm**: "I intend to stay calm and centered, managing my energy and saying no to commitments that don't align with my well-being."
- **Practice Generosity**: "I intend to give from the heart, sharing my time, kindness, or resources in ways that feel genuine and meaningful."
- **Be Present**: "I intend to fully engage in each moment, letting go of distractions and savoring the holiday experience as it unfolds."

Integrating Your Intentions into Daily Life

Once you've set your intentions, the next step is to incorporate them into your daily routine. Intentions are most effective when they're woven into your everyday experiences rather than reserved for special occasions. Here are some ideas for bringing your intentions to life during the holidays.

1. **Begin Each Day with a Reminder**: Start your morning by revisiting your intentions. Take a few deep breaths, focus on your intentions, and imagine how they might shape your day. Setting an intention first

thing in the morning can help you approach the day with clarity and purpose.

2. **Use Your Intentions as a Guide for Decisions**: When faced with choices — whether it's attending a gathering, purchasing a gift, or planning an activity — use your intentions as a filter. Ask yourself if the decision aligns with your values and goals for the season. If it does, proceed; if not, consider a different approach that feels truer to your intentions.

3. **Create Simple Rituals Around Your Intentions**: Rituals can be a beautiful way to honor your intentions. For instance, if your intention is gratitude, create a daily gratitude practice by writing down three things you're thankful for each evening. If your intention is connection, plan a weekly coffee or phone call with a loved one to deepen your bonds.

4. **Pause and Reflect Throughout the Day**: Holidays can be busy, so it's helpful to build in small moments to pause and reconnect with your intentions. When you feel stressed or distracted, take a few moments to breathe and remind yourself of your intentions. This simple pause can help you return to a place of calm and clarity.

5. **Celebrate Small Wins**: Recognize the moments when you've lived in alignment with your intentions. Celebrating these small wins reinforces your commitment to your goals and helps you feel fulfilled and motivated. Whether it's a mindful gathering, a heartfelt conversation, or a calm response to a stressful situation, each alignment with your intentions is worth acknowledging.

Letting Go of Perfection

An essential part of setting intentions is recognizing that they aren't meant to create a "perfect" holiday. Rather, intentions help us stay grounded in what's meaningful, even when the holiday season brings surprises, changes, or challenges. Life is unpredictable, and perfection is an unrealistic goal. By focusing on intentions instead of outcomes, we give ourselves permission to embrace imperfection with grace and resilience.

For example, if you set an intention to cultivate calm but find yourself overwhelmed, it's okay to pause, regroup, and return to your intention without judgment. Intentions are there to support us, not to create additional pressure. The more we approach the season with flexibility and self-compassion, the more we can experience the holidays as a time of peace, presence, and joy.

Creating a Mindfulness Practice

In the midst of holiday busyness, incorporating a mindfulness practice into your routine can provide a much-needed anchor. Mindfulness, the practice of paying full attention to the present moment with an open and non-judgmental attitude, has been shown to reduce stress, improve mood, and increase emotional resilience — all benefits that can help us navigate the holiday season with greater ease. By creating a simple, accessible mindfulness practice, you can cultivate a sense of calm and presence that carries you through each day, helping you stay grounded even when the season's demands intensify.

This chapter introduces a variety of mindfulness practices, grounded in research, that can be integrated into daily life with minimal effort. The goal is not to add more to your to-do list but to offer tools for finding peace, reducing stress, and fully experiencing the beauty of the season.

. . .

Why Mindfulness Matters During the Holidays

The benefits of mindfulness are well-documented. Studies have shown that mindfulness practices can reduce stress, decrease symptoms of anxiety and depression, and improve emotional regulation. Practicing mindfulness has also been associated with lower levels of cortisol, the stress hormone, which can become elevated during periods of high tension, like the holidays. By cultivating mindfulness, we can interrupt the cycle of stress and create space for presence, gratitude, and joy.

Mindfulness can also enhance our ability to connect with others. When we're fully present, we're better able to listen, empathize, and engage meaningfully, which deepens our relationships and enriches our experiences with loved ones. In addition, mindfulness helps us tune into our own needs, so we're more likely to recognize when we're overextended, fatigued, or in need of a break.

Getting Started with a Mindfulness Practice

Creating a mindfulness practice doesn't require special equipment, extensive training, or hours of time. It's about bringing awareness into simple, everyday activities. Here are a few foundational practices to help you begin:

1. **Mindful Breathing**: One of the simplest and most effective mindfulness practices is mindful breathing. This practice involves focusing your attention on each inhale and exhale, allowing you to center yourself in the present moment. Research shows that slow, deep breathing activates the parasympathetic nervous system, which promotes relaxation and reduces stress.

- *How to Practice*: Sit comfortably and close your eyes if that feels comfortable. Breathe in slowly through your nose, filling your lungs, and then exhale fully through your mouth. Count each breath to ten, then start over. When your mind wanders, gently bring it back to the breath. Even just five minutes of mindful breathing each day can help reset your nervous system and cultivate calm.
2. **Body Scan**: A body scan involves directing attention to each part of your body, noticing any sensations, tension, or relaxation. Research on body scan practices shows they can improve body awareness, reduce physical tension, and promote relaxation. This practice can be particularly helpful when feeling overwhelmed or disconnected from your body.
    - *How to Practice*: Start at your feet, noticing any sensations. Gradually work your way up through your legs, torso, arms, and head. If you notice any tension, imagine breathing into that area, then exhale and allow the tension to release. A body scan can take as little as five minutes or as long as thirty, depending on how much time you have.
3. **Mindful Walking**: Mindful walking is an excellent way to ground yourself, especially if you're feeling stressed or overstimulated. Walking mindfully helps bring awareness to physical sensations, the environment, and the rhythm of your body, which can calm your mind and elevate your mood. Studies have shown that mindful walking can improve both mental and physical well-being by reducing stress and increasing energy levels.

- *How to Practice*: As you walk, focus on each step. Notice how your feet connect with the ground, the sensation of the air on your skin, and the rhythm of your movements. If you're outside, take in the sights and sounds around you. When your mind wanders, gently bring it back to the sensation of walking. Even a five-minute walk can provide a refreshing break and help you return to your day with a clearer mind.

4. **Loving-Kindness Meditation**: This mindfulness practice is focused on cultivating compassion, both for yourself and others. Loving-kindness meditation has been shown to improve emotional resilience, increase feelings of social connection, and reduce stress and anxiety.
    - *How to Practice*: Sit comfortably, close your eyes, and take a few deep breaths. Begin by focusing on yourself, repeating phrases like, "May I be happy, may I be healthy, may I be safe." Gradually extend these phrases to others, starting with loved ones and eventually including people you don't know well or may have challenges with. This practice can take as little as five minutes and has a powerful impact on emotional well-being and relationships.

5. **Gratitude Practice**: A gratitude practice involves reflecting on things you're thankful for, which shifts your focus from what's lacking to what's present and positive. Research shows that cultivating gratitude can improve mood, reduce stress, and enhance overall well-being.
    - *How to Practice*: Each day, take a few minutes to write down or mentally note three things you're grateful for. Try to focus on specifics, like "the

warmth of my morning coffee" or "a kind word from a friend." You can practice gratitude in the morning to set a positive tone for the day or in the evening to reflect on meaningful moments.

Integrating Mindfulness into Holiday Activities

Mindfulness doesn't have to be limited to formal practice sessions; it can also be woven into everyday holiday activities. By bringing mindful awareness to tasks like gift-wrapping, cooking, or decorating, you can transform them from chores into moments of calm and enjoyment. Here are a few ideas:

1. **Mindful Gift-Wrapping**: Rather than rushing through wrapping presents, try to be fully present with the process. Notice the texture of the paper, the sound of the scissors, the way the ribbon feels in your hands. By focusing on each step, you'll likely find the experience more enjoyable and less hurried.
2. **Mindful Eating**: The holidays are full of delicious foods, and eating mindfully can enhance your enjoyment. Take small bites, chew slowly, and savor each flavor. Research has shown that mindful eating can improve digestion, increase satisfaction, and prevent overeating by helping you tune into your body's hunger and fullness cues.
3. **Mindful Decorating**: When decorating, engage all your senses. Notice the colors, textures, and smells of the decorations. Put on music that brings you joy, and let yourself fully experience the act of creating a holiday atmosphere. Decorating mindfully can help you feel more connected to your environment and the

season's spirit.
4. **Mindful Listening in Conversations**: When spending time with loved ones, practice mindful listening by giving your full attention to the other person. Put away distractions, maintain eye contact, and focus on their words without planning your response. Mindful listening enhances empathy and strengthens bonds, helping you connect more deeply with those around you.

Making Mindfulness a Consistent Practice

Establishing consistency with mindfulness doesn't have to be complicated. Here are some tips to help make mindfulness a regular part of your holiday routine:

- **Start Small**: Begin with just a few minutes a day and gradually increase as it feels comfortable. Even a short practice can have significant benefits.
- **Set a Daily Reminder**: Create a routine by setting a specific time each day for mindfulness. Whether it's first thing in the morning, during lunch, or before bed, having a designated time can help build consistency.
- **Pair Mindfulness with Existing Habits**: Try integrating mindfulness into your regular routines. For example, practice mindful breathing while brushing your teeth, do a body scan before going to sleep, or take a few mindful breaths when waiting in line.
- **Be Kind to Yourself**: It's natural for the mind to wander, and there's no "perfect" way to practice mindfulness. Approach each session with a sense of curiosity and kindness, letting go of self-criticism.

Mindful Planning

Planning for the holidays can feel like navigating a maze of tasks, events, and responsibilities. From gift shopping and meal planning to scheduling gatherings, it's easy to become overwhelmed by the sheer number of things that need to be done. However, by taking a mindful approach to planning, we can transform these tasks from sources of stress into intentional, enjoyable activities that align with our values and priorities.

Mindful planning means approaching holiday preparations with calm, purpose, and awareness. Instead of rushing through tasks or getting caught up in a frenzy of last-minute decisions, we can make thoughtful choices that prioritize our well-being and reflect what truly matters. This chapter offers practical tips for applying mindfulness to holiday planning, helping you reduce stress and cultivate a season that feels manageable and meaningful.

Why Mindful Planning Matters

Planning mindfully allows us to create a holiday experience that aligns with our values, reduces unnecessary stress, and enables us to be fully present with ourselves and others. Research shows that proactive planning, especially when combined with mindful awareness, can help reduce anxiety, improve time management, and foster a greater sense of control. By approaching holiday tasks with intention, we're better equipped to avoid burnout, manage expectations, and stay connected to the joy and purpose of the season.

Mindful planning also encourages us to set boundaries around our time and energy, helping us prioritize quality over quantity and avoid overextending ourselves. This approach can lead to a holiday experience that feels fulfilling, manageable, and true to our intentions.

Tips for Mindful Holiday Planning

1. **Set Priorities Before You Begin**: Before diving into holiday tasks, take a moment to define your priorities. What aspects of the holiday are most important to you? Is it spending time with family, cooking a special meal, or giving meaningful gifts? By identifying your top priorities, you can focus your time and energy on what matters most, letting go of tasks that don't align with your values.
    - *How to Practice*: Write down a list of your top three holiday priorities and keep them somewhere visible. Use this list as a guide for making decisions about where to invest your time, money, and energy.
2. **Break Tasks into Manageable Steps**: The holiday season can feel overwhelming because of the sheer number of things to do. Breaking larger tasks into smaller, manageable steps can make planning feel more achievable. Research suggests that breaking tasks down reduces cognitive load and increases motivation by providing a clear roadmap.
    - *How to Practice*: Instead of tackling "holiday shopping" as one big task, break it down into smaller steps, such as setting a budget, creating a list, researching items, and purchasing gifts. Schedule these steps over time to avoid last-minute pressure.

3. **Set a Realistic Budget**: Financial strain is a common source of holiday stress. By setting a realistic budget and sticking to it, you can reduce anxiety and make mindful spending decisions that align with your financial situation and values. Studies show that budgeting can help reduce stress by providing a sense of control and structure.
    - *How to Practice*: Set a holiday budget that includes categories like gifts, food, decorations, and travel. Track your spending, and regularly check in with yourself to ensure you're staying within your limits. If possible, consider alternative, budget-friendly options like homemade gifts, potluck-style gatherings, or experiential gifts.
4. **Use a Calendar to Space Out Activities**: Scheduling holiday tasks across several weeks can help prevent last-minute rushes and reduce overall stress. By spacing out activities, you can avoid overwhelming yourself and create time to enjoy each task without feeling pressured. Research indicates that proactive scheduling promotes time management and helps prevent burnout.
    - *How to Practice*: Mark holiday-related tasks on your calendar, from gift shopping and meal planning to social events. Aim to complete high-stress activities, like shopping, earlier in the season. Leave open spaces in your calendar for rest and spontaneity, allowing for a balanced schedule.
5. **Set Boundaries Around Commitments**: Social obligations and events are a significant part of the holiday season, but attending too many gatherings can lead to burnout. Setting boundaries allows you to

be selective about the events you attend, focusing on those that bring you joy and connection rather than obligation.
- *How to Practice*: Take time to consider each event invitation thoughtfully. Ask yourself if attending aligns with your holiday intentions and energy levels. Politely decline events that don't resonate with you, and don't be afraid to limit the time you spend at gatherings if you feel overstimulated or tired.

6. **Create a Plan for Gift Shopping**: Gift shopping can be one of the most stressful holiday tasks, but with mindful planning, it can become a thoughtful and enjoyable activity. Planning your shopping allows you to be intentional about your choices and reduces the pressure of finding last-minute gifts.
    - *How to Practice*: Start by making a list of people you want to give gifts to and brainstorming meaningful ideas for each person. Set a budget for each gift and stick to it. Consider shopping online to avoid crowds or choosing experiential gifts, such as a shared outing or a homemade treat, which often feel more personal and meaningful.

7. **Plan Meals Mindfully**: Holiday meals are an opportunity to connect with loved ones, but they can also be a source of stress if we feel pressure to prepare elaborate dishes. By planning meals mindfully, you can create a nourishing experience without overextending yourself.
    - *How to Practice*: Choose a few key dishes that are meaningful to you and feel achievable within your time and energy limits. Consider simplifying

recipes or asking family members to bring a dish to share. Focus on creating an enjoyable atmosphere rather than a picture-perfect meal, remembering that the purpose of the meal is to foster connection.
8. **Schedule "Unstructured" Time**: The holidays can be packed with activities, leaving little room for rest and reflection. By scheduling downtime, you create intentional space for relaxation, self-care, and enjoying the season in an unstructured way. Research supports the benefits of taking breaks, showing that rest periods can improve mood, energy, and focus.
    - *How to Practice*: Block out a few hours each week for unstructured time. Use this time to do something that brings you joy, whether it's reading, listening to music, going for a walk, or simply resting. Treat this time as a priority, allowing yourself to recharge amid the holiday activities.

Embracing Flexibility and Adaptability

Mindful planning is about creating a structure that reduces stress, but it's also important to stay flexible. Unexpected changes are inevitable during the holiday season, whether it's a last-minute schedule shift, a delayed delivery, or an unexpected guest. By embracing a mindset of adaptability, we can respond to these changes with greater calm and less frustration.

1. **Practice Non-Attachment to Outcomes**: Mindfulness encourages us to let go of rigid expectations and embrace the present moment as it is. When things don't go according to plan, practice

letting go of the ideal outcome and focus on the experience itself.
2. **Reframe Setbacks as Opportunities**: Instead of viewing disruptions as negative, consider them as opportunities for creativity and resilience. A meal that doesn't go as planned, for example, can become a fun story or a chance to improvise.
3. **Prioritize Your Well-Being Over Perfection**: Remind yourself that a "perfect" holiday isn't the goal. Your mental, emotional, and physical well-being are more important than achieving an idealized version of the season. Allow yourself to make adjustments as needed and recognize when it's time to slow down or change course.

Moving Forward

Mindful planning is about approaching holiday preparations with intention, flexibility, and purpose. By setting priorities, breaking tasks into manageable steps, and creating a balanced schedule, you can transform the season from a source of stress into an opportunity for joy, connection, and fulfillment. With a mindful approach to planning, you're better able to create a holiday experience that aligns with your values and nurtures your well-being.

In the chapters ahead, we'll continue exploring ways to integrate mindfulness into holiday traditions, gatherings, and self-care practices. Each aspect of the season presents a chance to approach with awareness, helping you cultivate a holiday that's both meaningful and manageable.

Remember, mindful planning isn't about perfecting every

detail but about creating space to be fully present in each moment. With thoughtful preparation and an open heart, you can enjoy a holiday season that brings peace, connection, and genuine fulfillment.

Chapter 3
Mindful Gift-Giving

G ift-giving is one of the most cherished holiday traditions, a way of expressing love, appreciation, and thoughtfulness. However, in recent years, the holiday season has become synonymous with materialism and consumerism, as we're encouraged to buy more, spend more, and give more. For many, the pressure to buy gifts can lead to stress, financial strain, and a sense of obligation rather than joy. This chapter explores how to approach gift-giving mindfully, shifting from quantity to quality and focusing on meaningful, thoughtful gestures that foster connection and appreciation.

Mindful gift-giving allows us to return to the heart of the tradition — showing love and care for others in ways that reflect our values and intentions. By rethinking how we give and focusing on gifts that encourage connection and joy, we can transform holiday shopping from a stressful obligation into an act of mindfulness, gratitude, and creativity.

Rethinking Gift Culture

The commercialization of the holiday season has given rise to a gift culture focused on quantity, competition, and often, excessive spending. Advertisements and social media can amplify feelings of inadequacy or pressure, suggesting that love is measured by the size, expense, or number of gifts we give. But as research shows, materialism is linked to lower life satisfaction, increased stress, and diminished happiness, all of which can undercut the true spirit of the season.

Mindful gift-giving encourages us to question this culture and approach the tradition in a way that feels more intentional. Instead of focusing on material goods or expensive items, we can shift our perspective toward gifts that truly resonate with the recipient and foster a deeper sense of connection. This approach isn't about giving less but about giving with purpose and authenticity, creating a holiday experience that feels more fulfilling and less stressful.

The Joy of Thoughtful Giving

A mindful approach to gift-giving centers on thoughtfulness rather than quantity. Thoughtful gifts don't need to be grand or expensive; they simply reflect a deep understanding of the recipient and an intention to bring them happiness. Research shows that gift-giving can bring joy to both the giver and the recipient, especially when the gift feels personal and meaningful.

Here are some tips for shifting from quantity to quality in your gift-giving:

1. **Focus on Personalization**: Think about the recipient's personality, interests, and values. What brings them joy? What do they love to do in their free time? Personalized gifts, such as a book by their favorite author, a kitchen gadget they've been wanting, or a photo album of shared memories, show that you truly see and appreciate them.
2. **Consider "Less but Better"**: Instead of feeling pressured to buy multiple items, consider choosing one thoughtful gift that holds personal meaning. For example, a handwritten letter, a cozy blanket, or a framed photo of a meaningful moment can carry more emotional weight than a collection of smaller, less personal items. Studies suggest that people tend to value gifts with emotional resonance more than purely functional ones.
3. **Prioritize Quality Time**: Sometimes, the most meaningful gift you can give is your presence. Consider planning a shared experience with your loved ones, like a lunch date, a nature hike, or a movie night at home. Experiences create lasting memories

and strengthen relationships, often leaving a deeper impact than material items.
4. **Ask for Ideas**: It's okay to ask your loved ones what they'd like or need. While some may enjoy the surprise of a gift, others might prefer to receive something specific or practical. By asking for ideas, you can ensure your gift aligns with the recipient's needs or desires, creating a sense of mutual appreciation.
5. **Remember the Little Things**: Thoughtful giving doesn't always need to involve big gestures. Small tokens of appreciation, such as a favorite snack, a handwritten note, or a small act of service, can bring genuine joy to the recipient. Often, it's these little details that feel the most heartfelt and memorable.

DIY and Experience-Based Gifts

One of the most meaningful ways to approach gift-giving is through DIY and experience-based gifts. These gifts prioritize connection, creativity, and presence, encouraging both the giver and the recipient to engage more deeply with the act of giving. DIY and experience-based gifts are often more personal and memorable, allowing you to share a piece of yourself or create shared experiences with loved ones.

Below are some creative ideas for DIY and experience-based gifts:

1. **Handmade Gifts**: Crafting a gift by hand infuses it with a personal touch and shows the recipient that you've put thought and effort into creating something special just for them. Here are a few DIY ideas:

- **Customized Recipe Book**: Collect your favorite recipes or family recipes and organize them into a small, handmade book. Personalize it with notes or stories about each dish to make it even more meaningful.
- **Homemade Treats**: Baking cookies, making preserves, or crafting a batch of homemade chocolates can be a delightful gift. Package these treats in decorative jars or boxes for a beautiful, heartfelt presentation.
- **Personalized Artwork**: If you have a talent for painting, drawing, or calligraphy, create a piece of artwork or write a favorite quote for your recipient. Frame it or make it into a small card for a lasting keepsake.

2. **Experience-Based Gifts**: Experiences often bring more lasting happiness than material goods, as they create memories and opportunities for connection. An experience-based gift shows that you value spending time together and are invested in making meaningful memories. Here are some ideas:
   - **Tickets to an Event**: Consider giving tickets to a concert, theater performance, museum exhibit, or sporting event that the recipient would enjoy. This gift allows you to share an experience and create lasting memories.
   - **Class or Workshop**: Give the gift of learning by enrolling your loved one in a class or workshop. Choose something aligned with their interests, such as a cooking class, pottery workshop, or yoga session. Better yet, take the class together!
   - **Day Trip or Outing**: Plan a day out to a local attraction, nature spot, or nearby town. Create an

itinerary of activities or places you know they'd enjoy. This type of gift allows you to spend quality time together and explore something new.
3. **Gift of Service**: Acts of service can be incredibly meaningful, especially when tailored to the recipient's needs. This type of gift is less about material items and more about showing kindness and support. Here are some ways to offer a gift of service:
    - **Offer Help with Tasks**: Create a coupon book of helpful tasks, like babysitting, pet-sitting, home repairs, or cooking a meal. This is particularly meaningful for recipients who may appreciate extra support.
    - **Organize a "Chore-Free" Day**: Take care of the chores or responsibilities of a loved one for a day, allowing them to fully relax. Whether it's running errands, preparing meals, or tidying up, this gift can be a welcome relief during a busy season.
    - **Plan a Care Package**: For a loved one who may be going through a difficult time or simply needs a bit of pampering, assemble a care package with their favorite treats, books, and self-care items. Include a personal note or words of encouragement to lift their spirits.
4. **Charitable Giving in Their Name**: If the recipient values giving back, consider donating to a charity or cause they care about in their name. This is an especially meaningful gesture for those who already have what they need and would appreciate seeing their gift go toward making a positive impact.

Mindful gift-giving offers a path away from materialism and toward connection, thoughtfulness, and authenticity. By choosing gifts that reflect care and consideration, we can transform holiday shopping into a more intentional and joyful experience. Each mindful gift serves as a reminder of our love, respect, and appreciation, creating moments of genuine connection between giver and recipient.

As you approach gift-giving this holiday season, remember that the value of a gift lies in the thought, effort, and love behind it, not in its price or quantity. By focusing on meaningful, personal gestures, you can create a holiday experience that brings joy, fosters connection, and encourages a spirit of gratitude.

In the next chapters, we'll continue to explore ways to bring mindfulness into all aspects of the holiday season, from gatherings with loved ones to self-care practices. By bringing awareness and intention into each part of the season, you're setting the stage for a holiday that feels peaceful, fulfilling, and aligned with what truly matters.

Chapter 4
Finding Peace Amid Holiday Chaos

Family gatherings are a central part of the holiday season, bringing opportunities to reconnect, celebrate, and strengthen relationships. However, they can also bring their own set of challenges. For many, family time during the holidays can be complicated by longstanding tensions, unresolved conflicts, or clashing personalities. Emotions tend to run high, and the expectations of holiday cheer can sometimes amplify the stress of dealing with difficult dynamics.

This chapter delves into practical, mindful strategies for managing challenging relationships and maintaining your peace in family gatherings. Instead of being swept up in the potential stress, you'll learn how to set boundaries, stay grounded, and approach family interactions with compassion and self-awareness. By focusing on what you can control — your reactions, your intentions, and your mindset — you can navigate family dynamics with grace, making room for connection, respect, and a bit of holiday joy, no matter the circumstances.

Dealing with Difficult Family Dynamics

Family gatherings can bring a sense of warmth, tradition, and connection, but they can also bring up complex emotions and long-standing tensions. Navigating family dynamics during the holidays can be challenging, especially when there are unresolved issues, personality clashes, or conflicting values. Even when we approach these gatherings with the best intentions, family interactions can sometimes trigger stress or frustration.

In this chapter, we'll explore strategies for managing challenging relationships and staying centered during family gatherings. By practicing mindfulness, setting boundaries, and focusing on what you can control, you can create a foundation for a more peaceful holiday experience, even in the face of difficult dynamics.

Understanding Family Dynamics

Family dynamics refer to the patterns of interaction between family members, shaped by years of shared experiences, roles, and communication styles. While positive dynamics can create a sense of belonging and support, negative patterns — such as criticism, competition, or avoidance — can lead to stress, conflict, and resentment. Recognizing these patterns is the first step in understanding why certain interactions feel challenging and what you can do to approach them more mindfully.

It's also essential to remember that family dynamics are complex and often influenced by deep-rooted emotions. It's unlikely that long-standing patterns will change overnight. Instead, the goal is to stay centered, manage your own responses, and approach interactions with self-awareness and compassion.

Strategies for Managing Challenging Relationships

1. **Set Realistic Expectations**: Going into family gatherings with idealized expectations can lead to disappointment, especially if past interactions have been challenging. Instead of expecting a picture-perfect holiday, set realistic expectations. Recognize that each family member brings their own personality, perspective, and emotional baggage, which can lead to moments of tension. By accepting that some difficulties may arise, you can prepare yourself emotionally and respond more calmly.
    - *Practice*: Before the gathering, take a moment to reflect on what might be challenging and set a realistic intention for the day. For example, instead of aiming for complete harmony, set an intention to stay calm, be present, or avoid specific triggers.
2. **Establish Boundaries**: Boundaries are essential for managing difficult family dynamics and protecting your well-being. Setting boundaries isn't about shutting people out but rather about defining what is and isn't acceptable in your interactions. Boundaries can help you avoid conversations that feel draining, limit time spent with specific people, or protect you from criticism.
    - *Practice*: Think about the boundaries you need to feel comfortable. For instance, if a family member tends to bring up controversial topics, you might gently say, "I'd prefer not to discuss this today." You can also set limits on how long you stay or decide to take breaks if the environment feels overwhelming.

3. **Use Mindful Breathing to Stay Grounded**: Family gatherings can sometimes feel emotionally intense. When you notice yourself becoming anxious, frustrated, or defensive, try taking a few deep, mindful breaths. Research shows that slow, deep breathing can activate the body's relaxation response, reducing stress and helping you stay calm in the moment.
    - *Practice*: Before responding to a challenging comment or entering a stressful environment, take three slow, deep breaths. Focus on the sensation of the breath to ground yourself, then approach the situation with greater clarity and calm.
4. **Reframe Negative Interactions**: Sometimes, difficult family interactions stem from misunderstanding, old habits, or even stress. When someone's behavior feels triggering, try to reframe the situation with curiosity and compassion. Instead of taking things personally, consider that their actions may reflect their own insecurities, stress, or unmet needs.
    - *Practice*: When faced with a negative interaction, mentally reframe the experience by reminding yourself, "Their behavior isn't about me." Practicing empathy can help diffuse your emotional reaction and make it easier to respond calmly.
5. **Use "I" Statements to Communicate Effectively**: During family gatherings, it's easy for misunderstandings to escalate, especially when discussing sensitive topics. Using "I" statements can help you express your feelings without blaming or criticizing, which reduces the likelihood of defensiveness and conflict.

- *Practice*: If you need to address a sensitive topic, start with "I feel" statements rather than "you" statements. For example, instead of saying, "You're always so critical," try, "I feel hurt when I hear critical comments." This approach opens the door to constructive conversation and helps maintain a respectful tone.
6. **Limit Engagement with Certain Topics**: Family gatherings can sometimes bring up sensitive topics — from politics and religion to lifestyle choices — that lead to tension or discomfort. If you know certain subjects are likely to create conflict, be mindful about steering clear of them. Redirecting conversations to neutral or positive topics can help keep the atmosphere light.
    - *Practice*: If a conversation is heading in a challenging direction, gently shift the topic by saying, "Let's talk about something else," or ask a question to redirect the conversation, such as, "What's everyone's favorite holiday memory?"
7. **Take Regular Breaks**: Family gatherings can be intense, and it's okay to take breaks when you need them. Stepping away for a few minutes allows you to reset, process your emotions, and regain a sense of calm. Breaks can help you manage overwhelm, reduce tension, and prevent reactions driven by stress or frustration.
    - *Practice*: Plan short breaks throughout the gathering. Take a walk outside, find a quiet room, or even go to the restroom for a few minutes of solitude. Use this time to breathe, check in with yourself, and recenter before returning to the group.

8. **Let Go of the Need to Fix or Change Others**: It can be tempting to try to "fix" difficult family members or change long-standing dynamics, but this often leads to frustration. Recognizing that each person is responsible for their own behavior can help you let go of unrealistic expectations and focus on what's within your control: your own actions and responses.
   - *Practice*: When you feel the urge to correct or change someone's behavior, remind yourself, "I can't control others, but I can control how I respond." This mindset can help you let go of unnecessary tension and focus on maintaining your peace.

Staying Centered and Grounded During Family Gatherings

Maintaining inner calm in a challenging family environment requires mindfulness and self-awareness. Here are a few strategies to help you stay centered and grounded:

1. **Set an Intention Before the Gathering**: Before entering a family gathering, set an intention that reflects how you want to feel and act. For example, you might set an intention to "remain calm," "be kind," or "enjoy the positive moments." Setting an intention helps you approach the gathering mindfully, giving you a sense of focus and purpose.
2. **Create a "Mental Reset" Phrase**: A mental reset phrase, such as "It's okay," "I'm here to enjoy the moment," or "Let it go," can serve as a quick reminder to stay centered. Repeating this phrase silently to

yourself can help calm your mind and keep you focused on your intention.
3. **Stay Connected to Your Breath**: Throughout the gathering, use your breath as an anchor to stay grounded. If conversations become stressful or overwhelming, return your focus to the sensation of breathing. This simple practice helps you detach from the tension and return to a state of calm.
4. **Focus on What You Appreciate**: During challenging moments, try to bring your attention to the aspects of the gathering that bring you joy, whether it's seeing loved ones, sharing a meal, or being part of a tradition. Shifting your focus to what you appreciate can help soften tension and make the experience more enjoyable.
5. **Have an Exit Plan**: If you know that extended family gatherings are particularly challenging, have an exit plan in place. Decide in advance how long you'll stay, and give yourself permission to leave when you feel it's best for your well-being. Letting yourself leave before reaching a point of exhaustion can help you end the gathering on a positive note.

Mindful Communication

The holidays bring together people from different backgrounds, experiences, and perspectives, making it a time of both connection and, sometimes, tension. Family gatherings, reunions with friends, and even workplace celebrations can bring up sensitive topics and emotional dynamics. Mindful communication can be a powerful tool for navigating these interactions, helping us stay calm, compassionate, and grounded even during stressful or emotionally charged moments.

Mindful communication involves being fully present, listening with empathy, and responding with thoughtfulness rather than reactivity. This chapter explores techniques for practicing mindful communication, offering strategies for staying centered, keeping conversations constructive, and cultivating empathy. By approaching conversations with intention and awareness, we can strengthen our connections, avoid misunderstandings, and create a holiday experience rooted in respect and understanding.

The Basics of Mindful Communication

Mindful communication is a practice of being intentional, aware, and respectful in our interactions with others. It involves a combination of mindful listening, thoughtful speech, and emotional regulation. When we communicate mindfully, we create space for authentic connection, understanding, and empathy, even in challenging situations.

Research on mindfulness and communication shows that mindful communication can reduce conflict, enhance empathy, and improve relationships. By being present and non-judgmental, we're better able to respond to others without impulsivity or defensiveness, which allows for more productive and compassionate conversations.

Key Techniques for Mindful Communication

1. **Practice Active Listening**: One of the most fundamental aspects of mindful communication is active listening. Instead of focusing on what you'll say next or judging what the other person is saying, practice giving your full attention. This helps the other

person feel heard and respected, which can diffuse tension and foster connection.
    - *How to Practice*: As you listen, make eye contact, nod to show understanding, and avoid interrupting. Try to listen without planning your response or forming judgments. If your mind wanders, gently bring your focus back to the speaker's words.
2. **Pause Before Responding**: In emotionally charged conversations, it's natural to react quickly, especially if we feel defensive or misunderstood. Taking a brief pause before responding allows us to consider our words and respond thoughtfully rather than impulsively. Research suggests that pausing before reacting can reduce conflict and enhance self-regulation.
    - *How to Practice*: When someone says something that triggers an emotional reaction, take a deep breath and pause before responding. This gives you a moment to assess your feelings, choose your words, and respond calmly rather than reactively.
3. **Use "I" Statements to Express Yourself**: Communicating with "I" statements, such as "I feel" or "I need," helps you express your feelings without blaming or criticizing others. This approach can prevent defensiveness and keep the conversation respectful. "I" statements also encourage introspection, helping you focus on your own experience rather than placing blame on the other person.
    - *How to Practice*: Instead of saying, "You always interrupt me," try, "I feel unheard when I'm interrupted." This small shift in language can

make a significant difference, reducing defensiveness and opening the door to a more constructive conversation.

4. **Acknowledge Emotions Without Judgment**: Emotions often arise during holiday conversations, whether it's joy, nostalgia, frustration, or resentment. Acknowledging your emotions and the emotions of others without judgment allows you to respond with compassion. Recognizing emotions as natural responses rather than signs of conflict helps keep the conversation constructive and caring.
    - *How to Practice*: If you sense tension, either in yourself or in someone else, take a moment to acknowledge it. You might think, "I'm feeling frustrated right now," or "They seem upset." By observing emotions without labeling them as "good" or "bad," you create a space where both you and the other person can feel heard and understood.

5. **Ask Open-Ended Questions**: Open-ended questions encourage dialogue, helping others share their thoughts and feelings more fully. Instead of asking yes-or-no questions, which can shut down conversation, try questions that begin with "how," "what," or "tell me about." Open-ended questions show genuine interest and curiosity, making the other person feel valued.
    - *How to Practice*: Instead of asking, "Did you like the meal?" try, "What was your favorite part of the meal?" This small change invites a deeper response and can lead to a more meaningful exchange.

6. **Validate the Other Person's Perspective**: Even if you don't agree with someone's opinion or perspective, showing validation and empathy can go a long way in maintaining a respectful, positive interaction. Validation doesn't mean agreeing; it simply means acknowledging that their perspective is valid to them. This creates an atmosphere of respect and helps prevent arguments from escalating.
    - *How to Practice*: If someone shares an opinion you disagree with, try saying, "I can see why you feel that way," or, "I understand that this is important to you." Validation demonstrates respect and shows that you're willing to listen, even if you don't share the same view.
7. **Stay Aware of Non-Verbal Cues**: Communication isn't just about words; non-verbal cues like body language, facial expressions, and tone of voice play a significant role in how our message is received. Mindful communication involves staying aware of these cues, both in yourself and in others. Positive body language, such as maintaining an open posture or smiling, can create a sense of warmth and openness.
    - *How to Practice*: Notice your posture, facial expressions, and gestures during conversations. Try to maintain an open posture, make eye contact, and use a calm, gentle tone of voice. Likewise, observe the non-verbal cues of the person you're speaking with to gain insight into how they're feeling.

Handling Difficult Conversations Mindfully

Holiday gatherings sometimes bring up sensitive topics, whether it's family dynamics, politics, religion, or lifestyle choices. When conversations turn difficult, practicing mindful communication can help you stay calm, prevent escalation, and keep the focus on mutual respect.

1. **Set Boundaries Around Sensitive Topics**: If you know certain topics are likely to lead to conflict, consider setting boundaries in advance. You might gently steer the conversation away from topics that feel too personal or emotional, or agree with family members to avoid specific subjects during the gathering.
    - *How to Practice*: If a sensitive topic comes up, say, "I'd prefer not to discuss this right now," or, "Let's focus on enjoying our time together." Setting a boundary early can prevent tension from escalating and allow everyone to feel more comfortable.
2. **Respond to Criticism with Curiosity**: Receiving criticism can be challenging, especially when it feels unwarranted. Instead of reacting defensively, try responding with curiosity by asking questions or seeking clarification. This approach can help you understand the other person's perspective and prevent misunderstandings.
    - *How to Practice*: If someone criticizes you, try saying, "Can you help me understand why you feel that way?" or, "I'd like to understand your perspective better." By responding with curiosity, you can turn the conversation into an opportunity for growth rather than conflict.

3. **Use Gentle Humor to Diffuse Tension**: Humor, when used mindfully, can lighten the mood and relieve tension during challenging moments. A lighthearted comment or shared laugh can diffuse defensiveness and help everyone relax. However, it's essential to be sensitive to the situation and ensure that humor is used constructively, not at anyone's expense.
    - *How to Practice*: If the conversation becomes heated, try making a lighthearted remark or sharing a funny memory to shift the focus. Humor can serve as a bridge, reminding everyone that the gathering is meant to be a time of enjoyment.
4. **Know When to Walk Away**: Sometimes, despite our best efforts, a conversation may feel too difficult to continue. Knowing when to walk away is an important part of mindful communication. Taking a break or excusing yourself from the conversation allows you to regain composure and prevent further tension.
    - *How to Practice*: If a conversation becomes overwhelming, politely excuse yourself by saying, "I'm going to take a quick break," or, "Let's take a pause and come back to this later." Walking away doesn't mean giving up; it's a way to protect your peace and manage the situation with grace.

Creating Space for Yourself

The holiday season often brings a whirlwind of activities, from gatherings and parties to gift exchanges and travel plans. With so many commitments, it's easy to lose sight of your own needs, leaving you feeling drained and overstretched. But creating space for yourself — prioritizing self-care, setting boundaries, and scheduling alone time — is essential for maintaining both physical and emotional well-being. Taking time to recharge isn't selfish; it's necessary for showing up fully and mindfully in all areas of your life.

This chapter explores the importance of creating space for yourself during the holiday season. By setting boundaries, practicing self-care, and carving out quiet moments, you can experience the holidays with more energy, balance, and joy. When you take care of yourself, you're better able to engage with others from a place of calm and authenticity, making the season more fulfilling for you and those around you.

The Importance of Self-Care During the Holidays

Self-care during the holiday season is crucial, yet it's often the first thing to be sacrificed amid the hustle and bustle. Studies show that engaging in regular self-care practices can reduce stress, improve mood, and boost resilience. Without it, we can quickly become overwhelmed, experiencing burnout, fatigue, and even resentment toward holiday obligations.

Self-care is about recognizing your needs, honoring them, and giving yourself permission to take breaks or ask for support when necessary. By integrating self-care practices into your holiday routine, you're investing in your well-being, allowing yourself to approach the season with greater presence and peace.

Strategies for Prioritizing Self-Care

1. **Set Boundaries Around Social Commitments**: The holidays often come with a packed schedule of events, from family dinners to office parties. While these gatherings can be enjoyable, too many can lead to social burnout. Setting boundaries allows you to choose which events feel

most meaningful and decline those that feel obligatory or draining.
- *How to Practice*: Before the holiday season begins, review your calendar and decide on the number of gatherings you're comfortable attending. Politely decline invitations that don't align with your energy or priorities, and give yourself permission to leave gatherings early if needed. By setting limits, you can protect your energy and make room for moments of quiet.

2. **Schedule Alone Time to Recharge**: Carving out moments of solitude during the holidays can provide a vital reset, allowing you to recharge amid the busyness. Whether it's a quiet morning walk, an hour with a book, or simply sitting in silence, alone time gives you space to reconnect with yourself and find peace.
    - *How to Practice*: Block out specific times on your calendar for solo activities, and treat these appointments as non-negotiable. Protect this time as you would any other commitment, allowing yourself to relax and recharge without interruption.

3. **Engage in Restorative Activities**: Restorative activities like reading, meditation, journaling, or taking a warm bath can help you unwind and release tension. These activities create a sense of calm, helping you return to the holiday season with a refreshed mind and body. Research shows that even a few minutes of quiet relaxation can improve mood, decrease anxiety, and increase resilience.
    - *How to Practice*: Choose one or two restorative activities that resonate with you, and incorporate

them into your daily or weekly routine. If possible, set up a designated space in your home for these activities, such as a cozy reading nook or a meditation corner. Creating a ritual around these practices can help you establish a self-care habit.

4. **Listen to Your Body's Needs**: With the abundance of holiday treats, late nights, and busy schedules, it's easy to overlook your body's needs. Practicing mindfulness with your physical health — from eating nourishing foods to getting adequate sleep — helps you stay energized and prevents the physical burnout that can accompany holiday stress.
    - *How to Practice*: Pay attention to how your body feels throughout the day. If you're hungry, eat something nourishing; if you're tired, make sleep a priority. Incorporate gentle movement like stretching or yoga, and practice mindful eating by savoring each bite without rushing. Taking care of your physical health can have a profound impact on your mental and emotional well-being.

5. **Practice Saying No with Kindness**: Saying "no" can be challenging, especially during the holidays, when there's a sense of expectation to participate in every event and meet every request. However, saying no is a powerful way to protect your energy and honor your boundaries. When done with kindness, a "no" can be both respectful and empowering.
    - *How to Practice*: If you're asked to take on a task or attend an event that feels overwhelming, try saying, "I appreciate the invitation, but I'll have to pass this time," or, "Thank you for thinking of me, but I need some time to recharge." Practicing

polite refusals helps you establish boundaries without feeling guilty.
6. **Create a Daily "Unwind" Ritual**: Establishing a daily ritual for unwinding can help you transition from the busyness of the day to a state of calm relaxation. A simple evening routine — like lighting a candle, practicing gratitude, or taking a few deep breaths — can signal to your body and mind that it's time to rest.
    - *How to Practice*: Choose a few calming activities that bring you peace, such as listening to soothing music, stretching, or drinking herbal tea. Dedicate 10–15 minutes each evening to these activities, using them as a way to unwind and let go of the day's stresses. A regular unwinding ritual can improve sleep, reduce stress, and prepare you for the next day.

Setting Boundaries with Loved Ones

Setting boundaries is essential for self-care, especially when it comes to interactions with family and friends. The holidays often bring up expectations from others, whether it's pressure to host, give generously, or attend every gathering. Boundaries allow you to protect your well-being while still honoring your relationships. By communicating your needs openly, you can prevent resentment and create a holiday experience that feels balanced.

1. **Identify Your Boundaries in Advance**: Before entering family gatherings or social events, think about what boundaries you need to feel comfortable and supported. Do you need to limit the amount of time you spend with certain family members? Do you want to avoid specific topics of conversation? Identifying

these boundaries in advance can help you feel more confident about asserting them.
2. **Communicate Boundaries Clearly and Respectfully**: When setting boundaries, communicate your needs with clarity and respect. Use "I" statements to express your feelings, such as, "I need some time to recharge," or, "I'd like to avoid discussing this topic today." Clear communication helps prevent misunderstandings and ensures that your needs are honored.
3. **Be Consistent with Your Boundaries**: Consistency is key to establishing effective boundaries. If you communicate a boundary, follow through on it. For example, if you've decided to leave a gathering after two hours, stick to that limit. Consistency reinforces your boundaries and shows others that you're committed to honoring your well-being.
4. **Practice Self-Compassion with Boundaries**: Setting and maintaining boundaries can be challenging, especially if you're not used to asserting your needs. Be compassionate with yourself if it feels uncomfortable, and remind yourself that creating space for your well-being is a healthy, necessary practice. Each time you honor a boundary, you're strengthening your commitment to self-care.

Creating Space for Reflection

During the holiday season, it can be easy to get caught up in external activities and lose touch with your inner self. Setting aside time for reflection allows you to reconnect with your values, emotions, and intentions. Reflection can provide a sense of clarity, reminding you of what's truly meaningful and helping you approach the season with mindfulness and purpose.

1. **Set Aside Time for Journaling**: Journaling is a powerful tool for processing emotions, releasing stress, and gaining insight. Take a few minutes each day or week to write about your holiday experiences, your feelings, and any moments of joy or challenge. Reflecting on the season through journaling can help you stay grounded and foster a sense of gratitude.
2. **Practice Daily Gratitude**: Gratitude is a proven way to boost mood, reduce stress, and enhance overall well-being. By taking time to appreciate the small joys of the holiday season, you can shift your focus from what's overwhelming to what's meaningful. Research shows that practicing gratitude can improve mental health and increase resilience.
    - *How to Practice*: Each evening, write down three things you're grateful for. These could be simple moments, like a warm meal, a friendly conversation, or a cozy blanket. Focusing on gratitude helps cultivate a positive outlook and reinforces the season's true spirit.
3. **Engage in Mindful Meditation**: Meditation is a valuable tool for reducing stress, calming the mind, and finding inner peace. Even a few minutes of meditation each day can help you feel more centered, especially during the busyness of the holidays.
    - *How to Practice*: Find a quiet space, close your eyes, and take slow, deep breaths. Focus on the sensation of your breath, allowing any tension or stress to release with each exhale. If your mind wanders, gently bring your attention back to your breath. Meditation helps you cultivate a sense of inner calm and prepares you to approach each day with mindfulness.

Moving Forward

Creating space for yourself during the holidays isn't just a luxury — it's a necessity. By prioritizing self-care, setting boundaries, and making time for reflection, you're taking intentional steps to protect your energy and well-being. These practices allow you to engage more fully with the season, approaching each experience from a place of calm, presence, and authenticity.

In the next chapters, we'll continue to explore ways to bring mindfulness into holiday gatherings, gift-giving, and personal traditions, helping you craft a holiday season that reflects your values and honors your well-being. Remember, the more space you create for yourself, the more you can give to others from a place of genuine joy and peace.

Chapter 5
Mindful Eating During the Holidays

The holiday season is a time of celebration, connection, and, often, abundant food. Festive gatherings bring cherished family recipes, mouth-watering aromas, and a sense of nostalgia, making it all too easy to find ourselves reaching for just one more serving. Yet, the joy of these occasions doesn't have to come with a side of discomfort or guilt. By embracing mindful eating practices, we can fully savor each bite, avoid overindulgence, and cultivate a healthy relationship with holiday meals.

The Essence of Mindful Eating

Mindful eating is the practice of being fully present during the act of eating. Instead of consuming food on autopilot, you slow down, engage your senses, and truly experience each moment. This approach allows you to not only enjoy the flavors and textures of food but also to recognize your body's hunger and fullness cues. Mindfulness at the dinner table can make the difference between feeling nourished and satisfied, rather than uncomfortably full or regretful.

During the holidays, the temptation to overeat is amplified by an abundance of rich foods and the festive atmosphere. Traditional holiday dishes are often prepared with extra sugar, fat, and salt, which can make them highly rewarding to our taste buds. While there's nothing wrong with indulging, mindful eating can help you fully appreciate each dish without slipping into the common cycle of overindulgence followed by guilt. By savoring smaller portions, we get to enjoy the best parts of holiday meals and maintain a sense of balance and well-being.

Slowing Down to Savor

One of the simplest yet most impactful ways to practice mindful eating is to slow down. Many of us eat quickly, which can lead to mindless eating and overconsumption before our body has had the chance to register fullness. Research suggests that it can take up to 20 minutes for your brain to recognize that you're full. By taking a few deep breaths before you begin eating and putting down your fork between bites, you allow your body the time it needs to communicate with you. This can make each bite more satisfying and prevent the common habit of eating beyond fullness.

During holiday meals, try to resist the urge to rush. Engage in conversation, take a moment to enjoy the presentation of the food, and give yourself the opportunity to appreciate each flavor. Eating slowly can heighten your sensory experience, making smaller portions feel more satisfying and allowing you to feel grateful for each part of the meal.

Listening to Your Hunger and Fullness Cues

Hunger and fullness cues are the body's natural signals to guide when, what, and how much to eat. Practicing mindfulness helps you tune into these cues, enabling you to make more intuitive food choices. Before you begin eating, pause and ask yourself: *Am I truly hungry, or am I eating because of tradition, social pressure, or even stress?* Holiday gatherings often revolve around food, and it's easy to feel compelled to eat whenever everyone else is, regardless of your own hunger level. Give yourself permission to participate in the holiday experience in a way that feels right for you, without the pressure to consume everything.

As you enjoy your meal, periodically check in with yourself. Notice the subtle changes in how food tastes and feels as you progress through the meal. Often, the initial bites are the most flavorful and satisfying; as you continue eating, the flavors may become less pronounced. Recognizing when your enjoyment starts to wane can be a helpful indicator that your body is becoming full. Honor your body's signals by stopping when you feel satisfied, rather than pushing yourself to finish every bite.

Practicing Nonjudgmental Awareness

Mindful eating is not about restriction or denying yourself

holiday treats. Instead, it's about cultivating a nonjudgmental awareness of what you eat and how it makes you feel. Guilt often accompanies indulgence, especially during the holidays when treats are abundant. However, guilt can lead to more impulsive eating and a strained relationship with food. Practicing nonjudgmental awareness means letting go of the internal commentary that labels certain foods as "bad" or "off-limits." It's about recognizing that it's natural and healthy to enjoy festive treats, while also staying attuned to your body's needs.

If you find yourself feeling guilty for enjoying a rich dish or dessert, gently remind yourself that there's no need to judge your choices. Instead, embrace the pleasure of each treat and recognize that the experience of enjoying holiday foods is a meaningful part of the season. By letting go of judgment, you can fully experience the joy of eating without negative emotions clouding the moment.

Strategies for a Mindful Holiday Meal

To help integrate mindful eating into your holiday celebrations, here are some practical strategies:

1. **Start with Small Portions**: Holiday meals often involve a variety of dishes, making it easy to feel overwhelmed by the options. Start with small portions of each item you'd like to try. This allows you to sample everything without overloading your plate. Remember, you can always go back for more if you're still hungry.
2. **Engage Your Senses**: Before taking a bite, take a moment to appreciate the visual appeal, aroma, and texture of the food. As you chew, notice the flavors and textures, allowing yourself to experience the full

sensory profile of the dish. This practice can enhance your enjoyment and satisfaction.
3. **Stay Hydrated**: Sometimes, thirst can be mistaken for hunger. Keep a glass of water nearby and take sips between bites. This can help you pace yourself and prevent overeating.
4. **Set Intentions**: Before the meal, set an intention to eat mindfully and enjoy the experience. Remind yourself that this time is about connection and celebration, not just about food. Setting an intention can provide a helpful anchor when temptations arise.
5. **Savor the First Few Bites**: Research suggests that the first few bites of a meal are often the most pleasurable. Focus on savoring these initial bites and see if they satisfy your cravings. This can reduce the urge to eat more than necessary.
6. **Pause Before Second Helpings**: Before reaching for seconds, take a few minutes to assess your hunger level. Engage in conversation, sip water, or enjoy a short break. This pause can help you determine whether you truly want more or if you're satisfied with what you've had.
7. **Practice Gratitude**: As you eat, take a moment to feel gratitude for the food, the people who prepared it, and the company you're in. Gratitude can enhance the experience and remind you of the joy that comes from shared meals, making the experience feel more fulfilling and balanced.

Gratitude for Nourishment

In the bustle of holiday preparations, it's easy to lose sight of the deeper meaning behind our meals. The holidays bring together friends, family, and loved ones around tables laden with festive dishes, but these moments hold more significance than the food itself. Embracing a mindset of gratitude for nourishment allows us to experience these meals as acts of connection, care, and shared joy. When we cultivate gratitude in meal preparation and consumption, every bite becomes more meaningful, transforming the act of eating into a mindful celebration.

The Role of Gratitude in Mindful Eating

Gratitude is a grounding practice that helps us stay present and connected to the moment. When we feel grateful, we're less likely to rush through our meals or consume mindlessly. Instead, we approach our food with a sense of respect and appreciation. This mindful perspective fosters a healthy relationship with food, replacing any tendencies toward guilt or overindulgence with feelings of contentment and satisfaction.

Gratitude for nourishment involves recognizing the journey of food from its source to your table. It includes the people who harvested, prepared, and shared it. This mindset can deepen your holiday meals into more than simply moments of indulgence—they become opportunities to acknowledge and appreciate the abundance around you. Each meal becomes a celebration of connection to the people, the earth, and the traditions that bring meaning to this time of year.

Honoring the Effort in Preparation

Holiday meals are often prepared with great care and attention, from choosing family recipes to spending hours in the kitchen. Recognizing the effort that goes into preparing a meal can transform how you experience it. For many families, holiday dishes carry memories, stories, and love passed down through generations. By consciously appreciating these efforts, you connect with the history and emotion embedded in each recipe.

When you sit down to enjoy a holiday meal, take a moment to acknowledge the time, energy, and love that went into its preparation. If you're the one cooking, reflect on the joy of preparing a dish for others to enjoy. This mindfulness can enhance your sense of gratitude and make each bite more fulfilling, knowing that you're part of a tradition that goes beyond yourself.

Gratitude for the Source of Food

Behind every dish on your holiday table lies a network of people, resources, and natural processes that made it possible. The vegetables, grains, and proteins that nourish us require the dedication of farmers, workers, and a healthy environment. Expressing gratitude for these sources helps you connect with a larger picture of nourishment that extends beyond the kitchen.

Consider reflecting on the journey of a few ingredients on your plate. Imagine the care taken to grow, harvest, and transport them. This small acknowledgment can help us realize how deeply interconnected our lives are with others and with the natural world. By recognizing the people and natural resources involved, we foster a sense of respect for the food we consume, encouraging a mindful approach to each meal.

Practicing Gratitude During the Meal

Gratitude doesn't have to be an abstract idea; it can be part of every meal. By incorporating gratitude practices into holiday meals, you can deepen your connection to the experience and to those you share it with. Here are some simple ways to bring gratitude to your table:

1. **Pause Before Eating**: Before diving into your meal, take a moment to pause. Whether you're dining alone or with others, spend a few moments reflecting on the food in front of you. You might silently thank the people who prepared it, acknowledge the farmers who grew the ingredients, or simply appreciate the abundance.
2. **Set an Intention**: Setting a gratitude-based intention can enhance your mindfulness as you eat. For example, you might set an intention to eat slowly, savoring each bite, or to stay present and engaged in the meal and the conversation. These intentions act as gentle reminders to appreciate the food, the people, and the moment.
3. **Express Gratitude Out Loud**: If you're dining with others, consider starting the meal by expressing gratitude together. This can be as simple as a few words of thanks for the food, the cooks, or the company. Sharing gratitude as a group can create a warm and connected atmosphere, setting a positive tone for the meal.
4. **Reflect on Past Holidays**: For many, holiday meals bring back memories of previous gatherings and loved ones. Take a moment to appreciate these memories and the people who may not be present. Acknowledging these connections helps you appreciate the role of family traditions and the sense of continuity they bring to our lives.
5. **Thank Yourself**: Especially if you've been busy with holiday preparations, acknowledge the effort you

put into creating a special experience for yourself and others. Recognizing your own contributions and care can foster a sense of self-compassion and remind you that you, too, are part of what makes the holiday season meaningful.

Finding Gratitude in Simplicity

Amidst the abundance of holiday feasts, we sometimes overlook the beauty of simple ingredients and uncomplicated dishes. Practicing gratitude doesn't mean you have to indulge in every delicacy; it's also about finding appreciation for the basics. This can be especially helpful if you're balancing holiday indulgence with wellness goals, as it encourages you to find satisfaction in lighter, nutritious options on the table.

Instead of focusing only on indulgent items, try to appreciate the simpler elements of the meal. The crispness of fresh vegetables, the flavor of a well-cooked grain, or the sweetness of a fresh piece of fruit can be just as satisfying when eaten mindfully. By appreciating the diversity and simplicity of your meal, you invite balance into your holiday eating and foster gratitude for all forms of nourishment.

Gratitude and Self-Compassion

The holidays can bring both joy and stress, and it's common to feel overwhelmed by social obligations, expectations, and even indulgences. Practicing self-compassion and gratitude during this season means giving yourself permission to enjoy without judgment. If you find yourself overindulging, gently remind yourself that it's natural and okay. Instead of dwelling on guilt, shift your focus back to gratitude for the experience and the opportunity to celebrate.

Self-compassion allows you to accept your choices and feel at peace with them. By practicing gratitude and self-compassion together, you'll be able to let go of rigid expectations, embrace the imperfections of holiday eating, and enjoy the season with an open heart. Each meal becomes an opportunity to practice kindness toward yourself, reinforcing a positive relationship with food and your body.

The Transformative Power of Gratitude

Gratitude has a unique ability to transform the way we experience food, relationships, and even ourselves. When you bring gratitude to the table, you invite a sense of warmth, mindfulness, and connection that goes beyond the physical act of eating. Gratitude reminds us that nourishment is about more than food—it's about cherishing moments, honoring efforts, and connecting with others.

This holiday season, allow gratitude to guide your meals. Use each moment of mindfulness and appreciation as a reminder that your holiday experience is not only about what's on your plate but also about who and what you cherish. Embracing this mindset can elevate your meals into meaningful celebrations, leaving you feeling both nourished and deeply connected to the spirit of the season.

Balancing Holiday Indulgence with Wellness

The holidays present a unique challenge when it comes to balancing indulgence with wellness. Rich foods, sugary desserts, and festive drinks are often central to holiday gatherings, and the season's emphasis on togetherness can lead to an abundance of celebratory meals. But embracing a balance between enjoying holiday treats and honoring your wellness goals can help you navigate the season with ease. Rather than feeling stressed or deprived, you can find joy in both indulgence and wellness by making intentional choices.

Embracing a Balanced Mindset

Balance is about finding a middle ground, allowing room for treats without guilt, and staying mindful of how food choices affect your well-being. This approach rejects the "all-or-nothing" mentality, which often leads to a cycle of overindulgence followed by restrictive eating. A balanced mindset acknowledges that health isn't determined by any single meal but rather by consistent habits and choices over time. By embracing this perspective, you can enjoy the holiday season to its fullest, savoring special foods while staying connected to what feels good for your body.

To cultivate a balanced mindset, focus on the joy of both nourishing and indulging. Recognize that wellness doesn't mean avoiding every treat but instead choosing foods and portions that make you feel energized and satisfied. By allowing yourself the freedom to enjoy holiday treats mindfully, you reduce the likelihood of overeating or feeling guilt after a meal. Each choice you make becomes a mindful act of self-care, ensuring that you feel both satisfied and well.

Choosing Nutrient-Rich Foods Alongside Holiday Treats

Holiday tables are often laden with rich, calorie-dense foods that may not be part of your usual routine. Balancing these treats with nutrient-dense foods allows you to enjoy the best of both worlds. Fruits, vegetables, whole grains, and lean proteins provide essential nutrients that help stabilize your energy levels, support digestion, and keep you feeling satisfied. By including nutrient-rich foods alongside indulgent dishes, you can maintain a sense of wellness without feeling deprived.

Consider filling half your plate with vegetables, fruits, or lean proteins at each meal. This can help balance the heavier options while still leaving room for treats. Colorful, fresh foods also bring a variety of flavors and textures, making your meal more satisfying. You might try adding roasted vegetables, a fresh green salad, or a hearty vegetable soup to the holiday spread. These dishes not only support wellness but also add variety to your meal, ensuring that you feel both full and nourished.

Setting Realistic Portions and Prioritizing Favorites

When surrounded by an array of delicious holiday dishes, it can be tempting to sample everything or serve large portions. Setting realistic portions and prioritizing your favorite foods can help you enjoy each meal without feeling uncomfortably full. By choosing a few items you truly want to savor, you allow yourself the pleasure of indulging without overloading your plate.

Start by scanning the options and identifying a few dishes that bring you the most joy or nostalgia. Serve yourself smaller portions of these favorites, savoring each bite without the pressure to finish a large plate. You can always go back for more if you're still hungry, but starting with modest portions gives you time to enjoy each flavor and prevents the feeling of overwhelm that often leads to overeating. Choosing a balance of favorite indulgent dishes with lighter, nutrient-dense sides can keep your energy steady and help you feel satisfied.

Staying Active to Support Physical and Mental Well-Being

Physical activity can be a valuable tool during the holiday season, helping you manage stress, digestion, and energy levels. Staying active doesn't mean hitting the gym daily or burning off holiday calories; rather, it's about finding ways to move your body that make you feel good. Simple activities like walking, stretching, or dancing can lift your mood, aid digestion, and provide a mental reset amidst the busy holiday schedule.

You might invite family or friends for a post-meal walk, or set aside a few minutes each day for gentle stretching or deep breathing exercises. These activities can help balance the mental and physical demands of the season, reducing stress and giving you a moment to reconnect with yourself. By incorporating movement into your holiday routine, you can support both your body and mind in feeling refreshed and grounded.

Practicing Gentle Boundaries

Holiday gatherings can sometimes lead to pressure to eat or drink more than you feel comfortable with. Whether it's well-meaning relatives urging you to try "just one more" serving or the sight of a lavish dessert spread, it's common to feel conflicted between honoring your preferences and participating in tradition. Practicing gentle boundaries allows you to maintain a sense of balance without feeling pressured or deprived.

One way to set gentle boundaries is to communicate openly with family or friends about your choices. For example, if a loved one encourages you to try a dish you're not interested in, thank them sincerely and let them know that you're enjoying your meal as is. Another strategy is to plan responses for common situations, such as politely declining seconds or opting for a lighter drink option. By being clear yet kind, you can maintain your wellness goals while still honoring your relationships.

Managing Stress and Emotional Eating

The holidays can be an emotionally charged time, filled with moments of joy but also with potential stressors, whether they stem from travel, family dynamics, or financial pressures. Many people turn to food as a source of comfort during stressful times, leading to emotional eating that can feel unbalanced. Recognizing and managing these stressors can help you make mindful choices and avoid using food to cope with emotions.

If you notice the urge to eat due to stress, take a moment to check in with yourself. Ask what you truly need at that moment—whether it's a break, a deep breath, or a comforting activity other than food. Practicing self-care through relaxation techniques like meditation, journaling, or breathing exercises can provide relief without the need for food as an emotional outlet. When you take care of your mental well-being, you create a foundation that makes mindful eating easier and more natural.

Planning for Post-Holiday Balance

One of the challenges of holiday indulgence is the tendency to feel pressure to "get back on track" immediately afterward. Planning for a balanced post-holiday routine can ease this transition and allow you to move forward without feelings of restriction or punishment. Instead of adopting an extreme or restrictive approach after the holidays, focus on gradually reintroducing your usual wellness habits.

You might start by planning nutrient-rich meals or engaging in physical activities you enjoy. Drinking plenty of water, incorporating fiber-rich foods, and returning to your regular sleep schedule can also help you feel more balanced. A gentle, sustainable approach to post-holiday wellness creates a positive mindset and allows you to enjoy holiday indulgences without the fear of "undoing" them.

Strategies for Balanced Holiday Indulgence

To help you enjoy the season while maintaining a sense of wellness, here are some practical strategies:

1. **Practice the 80/20 Principle**: Allow yourself to indulge in favorite treats while keeping 80% of your food choices nutritious and balanced. This principle helps you enjoy the season without feeling deprived or overindulgent.
2. **Alternate Alcohol with Water**: If you're enjoying holiday cocktails or wine, try alternating each drink with a glass of water. This not only keeps you hydrated but can also help you pace yourself and feel more mindful of your alcohol consumption.
3. **Eat Mindfully at Parties**: If attending a party with lots of tempting snacks, take a small plate and fill it with your chosen items rather than grazing. This helps you enjoy the food mindfully without eating more than intended.

4. **Get Creative with Healthy Holiday Recipes**: Explore nutritious holiday recipes that capture the flavors of the season without being overly heavy. Dishes like roasted root vegetables, seasonal salads, or fruit-based desserts can add a wellness-focused element to holiday meals.
5. **Honor Your Unique Preferences**: Remember that wellness looks different for everyone. Tailor your choices to what makes you feel your best, rather than following a one-size-fits-all approach. This helps you stay attuned to your needs and create a holiday experience that supports your well-being.

Balancing holiday indulgence with wellness is a journey that involves mindfulness, self-compassion, and intentional choices. By embracing a balanced approach, you can savor the joys of the season without sacrificing your well-being. This mindset allows you to feel both nourished and fulfilled, honoring the spirit of celebration while staying true to your wellness goals. Let this season be a time of joyful connection, both with loved ones and with yourself, as you discover the harmony between indulgence and mindful self-care.

Chapter 6
Mindful Holiday Traditions

H olidays bring a mix of warmth, nostalgia, and sometimes, stress and overwhelm. In our fast-paced lives, holiday traditions can feel like just another task on an already overflowing to-do list. However, when we infuse these moments with mindfulness, they can become meaningful pauses in time that genuinely enrich our lives. This chapter invites you to explore and even redefine your holiday traditions to align with what genuinely brings you joy and connection. Together, we'll look at ways to create new traditions, bring mindfulness into existing ones, and set aside time for meaningful reflection to make your holiday season truly fulfilling.

Creating New, Meaningful Traditions

Holiday traditions are like a patchwork quilt—pieces of memories and moments sewn together over years. Often, these routines are handed down, cherished, but sometimes followed without question. While many of these rituals bring warmth, nostalgia, and a sense of continuity, they can also become outdated or lose their magic, especially if they don't resonate with our present selves. At their core, traditions are meant to bring joy, connection, and meaning to our lives, but over time, they may become little more than a list of "must-do" tasks. In this chapter, we'll explore how you can bring intention and mindfulness to your holiday season by creating new traditions that align with your values, interests, and unique circumstances.

This process doesn't have to be overwhelming; even the smallest new practices can become beloved rituals. Small, mindful traditions often carry the most significance. A quiet evening spent watching your favorite holiday movie, an hour devoted to baking cookies from an old family recipe, or even volunteering at a local shelter—simple yet intentional activities—can bring you true joy. Once you identify those moments that light up your heart, you can begin to craft meaningful holiday traditions you look forward to each year.

Reflecting on What Matters

Creating new holiday traditions begins with introspection. Reflection allows you to understand which elements of your holiday season truly bring joy and connection and which ones feel more like obligations. This reflection helps bring clarity, giving you permission to embrace what resonates with you and gently let go of what doesn't.

To start, take some time to journal about your current holiday traditions. Ask yourself the following:

- What aspects of my holiday celebrations bring me genuine happiness?
- Are there traditions I follow only out of habit or obligation?
- Which activities do I feel excited about, and which ones feel stressful or overwhelming?

Through this journaling exercise, you may uncover traditions that no longer serve you. Maybe you feel pressure to attend a holiday gathering you've outgrown or to participate in gift exchanges that feel impersonal. Allow yourself to recognize that it's okay to make changes. Traditions aren't set in stone—they're meant to evolve with us. By letting go of the elements that no longer resonate, you make space for new traditions that genuinely align with your values and bring fulfillment.

Letting go doesn't have to mean abandoning beloved rituals entirely. Sometimes, small adjustments can make all the difference. If you love holiday gatherings but find large parties overwhelming, consider hosting a smaller, more intimate gathering with close friends or family. If traditional gift exchanges feel obligatory, explore alternatives, like giving thoughtful, handmade gifts or setting up a family outing instead. This gentle reflection can serve as a gateway to the intentional traditions you wish to cultivate.

Crafting Intentional Traditions

Once you've reflected on the elements of your holiday season that resonate with you, you're ready to craft new, intentional traditions. The following ideas encourage connection, creativity, and gratitude, allowing you to infuse your holiday with personal meaning and joy.

Mindful Gift-Giving

Gift-giving is often a cornerstone of holiday celebrations, yet it's easy to get caught up in the hustle and lose sight of its purpose. Instead of focusing on quantity, consider adopting a mindful approach to gift-giving. Thoughtful, intentional gifts carry far more meaning than expensive or elaborate items. You might find joy in making a handmade gift, such as a photo album, a knitted scarf, or a personalized playlist. Alternatively, experience-based gifts—like planning a special outing, sharing a meal, or writing a heartfelt letter—can create memories that last longer than material gifts. Mindful gift-giving brings the focus back to connection and allows you to give and receive from the heart.

This new tradition can also extend to family gift exchanges. For instance, you could agree to a theme, such as "books that changed our lives" or "homemade items," to inspire more personal and meaningful exchanges. Not only does this simplify the process, but it also allows each gift to tell a story, fostering a deeper sense of connection and shared joy.

Giving Back

For many, the holiday season represents a time of gratitude and generosity. Embrace the spirit of giving by making community service or charitable donations part of your holiday traditions. This might look like volunteering as a family at a local food bank, organizing a winter coat drive, or even contributing to a favorite charity in someone's honor. Creating a new tradition centered around giving back allows you to make a positive impact and reconnect with the true essence of the holiday season.

Family volunteer days can be especially meaningful. Whether it's serving meals at a local shelter or organizing holiday gift packages for those in need, shared acts of kindness can strengthen family bonds and instill values of empathy and compassion. Even small acts of generosity, like donating canned goods or making holiday cards for nursing home residents, can create a sense of purpose and remind us of the power of giving.

Celebrating Nature

Modern holiday traditions often keep us indoors—wrapped in the warmth of fireplaces, gatherings, and kitchen activities. But creating an outdoor tradition can bring a refreshing pause to the season's hustle and bustle. Spending time in nature can provide clarity, peace, and joy, whether it's a brisk winter walk, a gentle hike, or simply stepping outside to enjoy the fresh air.

An outdoor tradition could be as simple as a winter picnic, where you bundle up and bring hot chocolate and snacks to a nearby park, or a family hike to appreciate the quiet beauty of a snow-covered landscape. You could also start a tradition of collecting natural elements—like pinecones, holly branches, or winter flowers—to use in your holiday decorations. By reconnecting with nature, you create a grounding experience that allows you to pause and enjoy the beauty of the season.

Creating traditions that are rooted in joy and purpose allows the holiday season to transform into a time of genuine fulfillment, rather than an endless checklist of obligations. Reflecting on what brings you joy, letting go of the old habits that no longer serve you, and crafting meaningful traditions based on your values can help you celebrate in ways that truly resonate with you.

Remember that traditions don't have to be extravagant or complicated. Often, the simplest rituals carry the most meaning. A holiday movie night, a quiet evening walk, a family game day, or even a day set aside for reading by the fireplace can bring profound joy. These new traditions, grounded in mindfulness and intention, become gifts you give to yourself and your loved ones each year. Embrace the holiday season as an opportunity to slow down, savor the moments, and create memories that fill your heart.

With each holiday season, you'll be building a tapestry of mindful, joyful traditions that reflect who you are, who you want to become, and what matters most to you. Through this process, you reclaim the holidays as a time of warmth, connection, and celebration—true to your own heart.

Incorporating Mindfulness into Old Traditions

The holidays are filled with cherished traditions, handed down over generations or developed naturally over time. These rituals—whether it's decorating the tree, baking cookies, or gathering for a meal—hold a unique place in our hearts. Yet, in the rush of the season, it's easy to slip into autopilot, moving from one task to the next without fully appreciating the meaning or joy in each moment. By infusing mindfulness into our holiday traditions, we can transform these familiar activities into experiences of deep connection and fulfillment.

At their essence, holidays are about togetherness, gratitude, and celebration. Mindfulness allows us to experience these values more deeply, grounding us in the present moment and helping us savor each experience as it unfolds. In this chapter, we'll explore ways to engage all of our senses, practice gratitude, make space for pauses, and release the expectations that sometimes get in the way of our enjoyment. With these practices, we can breathe new life into old traditions, making them moments of true presence and joy.

Engaging the Senses

One of the simplest and most powerful ways to bring mindfulness to holiday traditions is to engage your senses. By slowing down and fully experiencing each moment through sight, sound, smell, taste, and touch, you can ground yourself in the here and now. For instance, if you have a holiday tradition of baking, allow yourself to savor each sensory detail. Notice the sweet, warm aroma of cinnamon and vanilla in the air, the softness of dough under your hands, the sound of your family's laughter or holiday music in the background, and the warmth of the oven as it fills the room.

Mindful engagement with your senses can turn even the most routine tasks into experiences of deep enjoyment and connection. Here are a few more examples to inspire you:

- **Decorating the Tree**: Instead of rushing to get all the ornaments on, pause to appreciate each one. Notice the colors, textures, and memories associated with each decoration. You might even make it a tradition to share a story about an ornament or why it's meaningful.
- **Holiday Meals**: Savor each bite by paying attention to the flavors and textures of your favorite holiday dishes. Appreciate the ingredients, the time it took to prepare them, and the enjoyment of sharing this meal with loved ones.
- **Gift Wrapping**: Focus on the sounds and sensations —the crinkling of wrapping paper, the snip of scissors,

the smoothness of a ribbon in your hands. Allow yourself to enjoy the process rather than rushing through it.

Engaging the senses with full attention can bring a richness to holiday activities, transforming them into moments of delight. These sensory details, often overlooked, are where memories are made. By noticing them, you deepen your connection to the experience, allowing you to truly savor the joy and beauty of the season.

Practicing Gratitude

Gratitude is at the heart of many holiday traditions, yet it's easy for its presence to fade into the background during busy holiday gatherings. Practicing gratitude intentionally allows us to stay connected to the spirit of the season, enhancing our appreciation for our loved ones and the celebrations we share.

One simple way to infuse gratitude into holiday traditions is to start gatherings or meals with a moment of shared appreciation. Take a few moments to reflect on the abundance around you—the food, the company, the laughter. Encourage everyone to share one thing they're grateful for. This can be as light-hearted or as profound as each person desires. Some might express gratitude for the meal, others for a supportive friend, and others for the memories created together. This practice creates a space for connection and sets a positive, mindful tone for the gathering.

Gratitude doesn't have to be limited to formal gatherings. You can also incorporate it into smaller, everyday holiday traditions. For example:

- **While Wrapping Gifts**: As you wrap each gift, take a moment to think about the person who will

receive it. Consider what you appreciate about them, and imagine the joy your gift might bring them.
- **In the Morning**: Start each day of the holiday season with a moment of gratitude. Take a few breaths and reflect on one thing you're grateful for that day, whether it's the sight of fresh snow, a friend's phone call, or a favorite holiday treat.
- **With Each Task**: Bring gratitude to even the smallest holiday tasks, like hanging lights or writing cards. Let each action be an expression of appreciation, acknowledging the joy these traditions bring to yourself and others.

Practicing gratitude reminds us to appreciate each moment of the holiday season, no matter how small. It shifts our focus from "getting things done" to noticing and valuing each experience, deepening our sense of fulfillment and joy.

Adding Breathing Space to Celebrations

Holiday events and traditions can be fast-paced, often leaving us rushing from one activity to the next. Incorporating mindful pauses, or "breathing space," into your day allows you to savor each moment and prevent the season from feeling overwhelming.

Taking mindful pauses is simple yet effective. For example, if you're decorating or wrapping gifts, periodically stop, take a few deep breaths, and take in the scene around you. Notice the colors, textures, and sounds, and allow yourself to feel grounded in the moment. These brief pauses allow you to step out of "doing" mode and enter "being" mode, where you can appreciate each moment as it unfolds.

Consider these mindful pauses throughout your holiday season:

- **Between Activities**: Instead of rushing from one event to the next, take a few minutes in between to rest. Sit down, take some deep breaths, and allow yourself a moment of calm before moving on.
- **During Gatherings**: If holiday gatherings feel overwhelming, step away for a moment to ground yourself. Take a few breaths outside, or find a quiet corner to check in with yourself before rejoining the group.
- **Before Meals**: Begin each meal with a moment of silence, allowing yourself to appreciate the food and the people around you. Take a few deep breaths, letting go of any stress or busyness and settling into the joy of sharing a meal.

Breathing space allows you to bring presence and calm into your holiday celebrations, creating a sense of ease. By making these pauses part of your traditions, you can approach the holidays with a grounded and peaceful heart, savoring each moment as it comes.

Letting Go of Expectations

Holiday traditions are rarely perfect, and sometimes, despite our best efforts, things don't go as planned. Part of incorporating mindfulness into old traditions is letting go of rigid expectations and embracing the season as it is, imperfections and all.

Mindfulness teaches us to approach each moment with an open, non-judgmental attitude. If the tree isn't decorated perfectly, or if the cookies turn out a little burnt, try to see these moments as opportunities for laughter and spontaneity. Letting go of the pressure for everything to go "just right" opens the door to joy, allowing you to be fully present, even when things don't go according to plan.

Here are a few ways to practice letting go of expectations:

- **Embrace Imperfection**: Remind yourself that the essence of the holidays isn't in perfection but in connection and presence. When something goes wrong, try to laugh and appreciate the uniqueness of the moment. Often, these "imperfect" moments become cherished memories.
- **Practice Compassion**: If you feel disappointed or frustrated, practice self-compassion. Acknowledge that it's okay to feel this way and gently remind yourself of the bigger picture. The true spirit of the season isn't about perfect decorations or ideal gatherings but about love, gratitude, and joy.
- **Reframe Expectations**: Instead of focusing on outcomes, focus on the experience. If things don't go as planned, ask yourself what you can learn from the moment or how you can still find joy within it. Reframing expectations allows you to stay adaptable and open-hearted.

Letting go of expectations frees you from the need for perfection and invites you to enjoy the holiday season as it truly is. It encourages a mindset of flexibility, openness, and gratitude, making space for real connection and joy.

Incorporating mindfulness into your holiday traditions can transform familiar activities into experiences of deep meaning and fulfillment. By engaging your senses, practicing gratitude, adding breathing space, and releasing expectations, you can turn old rituals into moments of true presence and joy.

With these practices, each holiday tradition becomes an opportunity to celebrate not just the season but the beauty of each moment. Let mindfulness guide you to a season filled with warmth, peace, and genuine connection—a holiday that leaves you feeling more present, fulfilled, and grateful.

Making Time for Reflection

In the midst of the holiday hustle, we're often swept up in a rush of activity. There are gifts to buy, meals to prepare, events to attend—all beautiful, but often overwhelming. In these busy times, taking a moment for reflection can be a powerful way to connect with the true meaning of the season. Reflection doesn't have to be a grand or time-consuming exercise. It can be as simple as a few minutes of journaling, a quiet morning spent with your thoughts, or a shared moment of appreciation with loved ones.

By pausing to reflect, we remind ourselves of the deeper values of the season—gratitude, kindness, connection, and love. In this chapter, we'll explore how to make time for reflection in small, meaningful ways, through daily journaling, shared reflection with loved ones, and a closing ritual to honor the season and set intentions for the new year.

Daily Reflections and Journaling Prompts

Setting aside just a few minutes each day to reflect can bring a sense of mindfulness and appreciation to the holiday season. When we take this time for reflection, we create space to let go of distractions and reconnect with what matters most to us. A daily practice of journaling or quiet reflection can become a grounding tradition, bringing moments of peace and clarity to each day.

If you're new to daily reflection, you may find it helpful to use journaling prompts as a guide. Below are a few prompts to support a mindful holiday season. Try reflecting on one question each day, writing down your responses, or simply meditating on them for a few moments. Each prompt invites you to connect with gratitude, presence, and kindness, cultivating a holiday experience rooted in mindfulness.

Daily Reflection Prompts:

1. **What am I most grateful for today?**
   - Reflecting on gratitude can shift our focus from what we lack to what we have. Even small moments of joy—like a warm cup of tea, a kind word from a friend, or the sight of holiday lights—can bring a sense of fullness and appreciation to the day.

2. **What traditions or moments from this season bring me true joy?**
   - Identify the activities, rituals, or people that truly light you up. Recognizing these moments can help you prioritize the experiences that bring the most meaning, allowing you to focus on what you love and let go of what feels obligatory or stressful.

3. **How can I show kindness or generosity today, even in small ways?**
   - This prompt encourages mindful giving, reminding you to offer kindness and compassion throughout the day. Small gestures, like helping a neighbor, giving a compliment, or sending a thoughtful message, can create a ripple of goodwill.

4. **What am I learning about myself during this season?**

- Holidays often bring up a range of emotions, from joy to stress to nostalgia. Reflecting on what you're learning about yourself—your needs, values, or even your boundaries—can lead to personal growth and a deeper understanding of your holiday experience.
5. **How can I bring a sense of peace and calm into today's activities?**
    - This question invites you to consider how you can approach each activity with calm and mindfulness. Perhaps it's by taking deep breaths, finding moments of stillness, or simply releasing expectations and focusing on being present.

By reflecting on these questions each day, you'll find it easier to stay aligned with what truly matters. You may even wish to keep your reflections in a holiday journal, one that you can revisit each year. Over time, you'll see how your intentions, experiences, and sense of joy evolve, creating a personal record of your mindful holiday journey.

Reflecting with Loved Ones

While personal reflection is powerful, sharing moments of reflection with loved ones can deepen the connection and joy of the season. The holidays offer unique opportunities to come together with family and friends, and a shared reflection can turn an ordinary gathering into a heartfelt experience. These shared moments remind us of the love and gratitude that bind us together, fostering a sense of togetherness that is the essence of the season.

There are many ways to incorporate shared reflection into your holiday celebrations. Here are a few ideas to get started:

- **Gratitude Sharing**: Before a holiday meal or gathering, invite everyone to share one thing they're grateful for. This simple act of gratitude can create a warm and positive atmosphere, encouraging everyone to focus on the abundance in their lives and the joy of being together.
- **Favorite Memories**: Another option is to take turns sharing a favorite holiday memory or something meaningful from the past year. This can be a light-hearted or deep reflection, depending on the tone of the gathering. Sharing memories invites everyone to reflect on joyful moments and fosters a sense of connection and appreciation for each other's experiences.
- **Reflection Circles**: For a more structured approach, you might create a "reflection circle" where everyone gathers in a comfortable space and each person shares a thought or answer to a chosen question. This could be as simple as "What has been the highlight of your year?" or "What brings you the most joy during the holidays?" Reflection circles can create a sense of intimacy and openness, encouraging everyone to connect on a deeper level.

Shared reflection is a beautiful way to honor the relationships that enrich our lives. Whether it's a moment of gratitude, a favorite memory, or a reflection on the past year, these moments of connection can bring a profound sense of meaning to the season.

Creating a Ritual of Closure

As the holiday season comes to an end, taking time for a ritual of closure can bring a sense of completion and gratitude. This closing ritual allows you to honor the experiences of the season and prepare your heart and mind for the new year ahead. Just as each holiday has its own beginning and unfolding, it's meaningful to create a gentle conclusion that lets you pause, reflect, and set intentions.

Here are a few ways to create a ritual of closure for the holiday season:

- **Season Highlights Journaling**: Spend an evening journaling about the highlights of the season. Write down your favorite moments, meaningful interactions, and any reflections or realizations that emerged. This practice allows you to capture the joy and gratitude of the season, and it becomes a beautiful record to revisit in future years.
- **Candle-Lighting Ceremony**: Light a candle as a symbolic act of closure and gratitude. As you light the candle, take a moment to appreciate the experiences and connections of the season. You might also take this time to set an intention for the coming year—a word or quality you hope to cultivate, like "patience," "creativity," or "kindness." This simple act can bring a sense of peace and clarity, helping you transition from the holiday season into the new year.
- **Writing a Letter to Yourself**: Write a letter to your future self, reflecting on what you've learned from the season and your hopes for the coming year. Share your thoughts, dreams, and intentions, and place the letter somewhere safe to open next holiday season. This practice allows you to capture the essence of your reflections and can serve as a meaningful reminder of your journey each year.

Creating a ritual of closure brings a sense of completeness to the holiday season. It allows you to reflect on what the season has meant to you, savor its highlights, and set mindful intentions for the year ahead. These moments of reflection help you carry forward the insights and growth from this holiday season, preparing you to welcome the new year with a heart full of gratitude and clarity.

Making time for reflection during the holiday season enriches each celebration, grounding you in mindfulness and helping you connect with the deeper meaning of this special time. Whether through daily journaling, shared moments with loved ones, or a simple closing ritual, reflection invites you to pause, appreciate, and savor each experience.

Let these reflections be your anchor amidst the holiday busyness, helping you create a season of joy, presence, and intention. By connecting with yourself and those around you, you transform the holiday season from a flurry of activities into a time of deep meaning and fulfillment, leaving you renewed and ready for the year ahead.

Chapter 7
Staying Present Amid the Hustle

The holiday season, with its festive cheer and excitement, often brings a whirlwind of activity. Between shopping, decorating, cooking, and attending gatherings, it's easy to feel like we're constantly racing to keep up. But what if, instead of rushing through each task, we could experience each moment with a calm and joyful presence? Staying mindful and grounded amidst the holiday hustle can transform stress into gratitude, enabling us to savor the season fully.

In this chapter, we'll explore simple practices to help you find presence even on the busiest days. From incorporating mindful moments into everyday activities, using breathing techniques to regain calm, and embracing gratitude, these practices will help you bring a sense of peace and joy to your holiday experience.

Mindful Moments Throughout the Day

During the holidays, it's easy to get caught up in a cycle of "doing"—checking off lists, meeting deadlines, and hurrying from one activity to the next. But even in the busiest times, it's possible to find mindful moments that bring us back to the present. These moments don't require you to stop what you're doing; instead, they allow you to approach each task with awareness, curiosity, and appreciation.

Here are some ways to find mindfulness in common holiday activities:

- **Shopping Mindfully**: Holiday shopping can be overwhelming, especially with crowded stores and long lists. Before you head out, take a few deep breaths and set an intention for your trip. Remind yourself to shop with kindness and patience. As you walk through the aisles, notice the colors, sounds, and energy around you. When selecting gifts, take a moment to reflect on the person you're shopping for, allowing yourself to focus on the joy of giving rather than the pressure to find the "perfect" gift.
- **Decorating with Presence**: Decorating your home can become a moment of creative expression and joy when done mindfully. Pay attention to each step—unpacking ornaments, hanging lights, or arranging wreaths. Notice the textures, colors, and

details that bring each piece to life. Decorating becomes less of a task and more of a sensory experience, grounding you in the moment and helping you appreciate the beauty of your surroundings.
- **Cooking or Baking with Intention**: Holiday cooking can be a flurry of activity, but it's also a chance to bring mindfulness into your day. Focus on the process—feel the ingredients in your hands, smell the spices, listen to the sounds of chopping and stirring. Cooking mindfully invites you to appreciate each step, turning a chore into a moment of creativity and care.
- **Traveling with Awareness**: If your holidays involve travel, it's easy to feel impatient and stressed. Try using travel time as an opportunity to practice mindfulness. While waiting, take slow breaths, observe your surroundings, or do a short meditation. Notice how your body feels, listen to the sounds around you, or simply observe your thoughts as they come and go. Traveling with mindfulness can help transform waiting and delays into moments of calm presence.

By infusing mindfulness into these daily activities, you bring a sense of presence to each experience, allowing the holidays to become a series of meaningful, joy-filled moments rather than a blur of tasks.

Breathing Techniques for Instant Calm

Amid the busyness of the holiday season, it's normal to feel moments of overwhelm. When stress builds, simple breathing techniques can bring instant calm, helping you refocus and reset. Breathing exercises are easy to practice anywhere—whether you're in the car, standing in line, or taking a quick break at home. Here are a few techniques to try whenever you need a moment of peace:

Box Breathing

Box breathing is a simple technique that brings calm by focusing on a steady rhythm of breaths. It's easy to remember and effective for grounding yourself in the present moment.

1. Inhale for a count of four.
2. Hold your breath for a count of four.
3. Exhale for a count of four.
4. Pause and hold for another count of four. Repeat this cycle a few times, visualizing each breath forming a "box" in your mind. As you breathe, imagine each inhale filling you with calm, and each exhale releasing any tension.

4-7-8 Breathing

The 4-7-8 breathing technique helps to release stress and bring the body into a state of relaxation.

1. Inhale quietly through your nose for a count of four.
2. Hold your breath for a count of seven.
3. Exhale completely through your mouth for a count of eight, making a soft "whoosh" sound.
4. Repeat the cycle three to four times. This technique slows your breath and activates the body's relaxation response, making it an effective tool for relieving stress in the middle of a busy day.

Mindful Breathing

Mindful breathing is one of the simplest forms of meditation and can be done in as little as a minute.

1. Close your eyes (if you're in a safe space to do so) and bring attention to your breath.
2. Notice the sensation of the air as it enters and leaves your body.
3. If your mind starts to wander, gently bring your focus back to your breath, observing each inhale and exhale without judgment. Mindful breathing can bring a sense of calm and clarity, helping you reconnect with yourself amidst the holiday hustle. Practicing it regularly, even just for a few moments each day, builds resilience to stress and strengthens your ability to stay present.

The Power of Gratitude and Presence

In the rush of the holidays, it's easy to lose sight of what the season is truly about. Practicing gratitude and presence allows us to reconnect with the joy and purpose behind each celebration. Gratitude, when practiced intentionally, has a transformative effect—it shifts our focus from what's lacking to what's abundant, helping us experience the holiday season with appreciation and joy.

Here are some simple ways to cultivate gratitude and presence throughout your holiday season:

- **Start the Day with Gratitude**: Begin each day by listing three things you're grateful for. They can be small or big—a cozy blanket, a good cup of coffee, a meaningful conversation. By starting your day with gratitude, you set a positive tone and carry a sense of appreciation into your daily activities.
- **Practice "Gratitude Pauses"**: During busy moments, pause for a few seconds and think of one thing you're grateful for in that moment. It could be

the laughter of a friend, the warmth of your home, or even the simple pleasure of having a moment to breathe. These "gratitude pauses" help you break out of the rush and reconnect with the joy of the season.
- **Be Present with Loved Ones**: Often, our minds are elsewhere during holiday gatherings, caught up in planning or worrying. Practicing presence with loved ones can deepen connections and create more meaningful memories. When you're with family or friends, focus on listening actively, noticing small details, and engaging fully in conversations. Let go of distractions and allow yourself to be fully present.
- **End the Day with Reflection**: Each evening, take a few minutes to reflect on the day's highlights. Consider what you enjoyed, what you're grateful for, and any meaningful moments you experienced. This simple practice not only fosters gratitude but also helps you stay present, carrying the essence of each day with you as you move forward.

Practicing gratitude and presence during the holidays invites us to savor the season in its fullness, finding joy in the smallest details and the simplest moments. Rather than focusing on what still needs to be done, gratitude allows us to appreciate what we have and be content with each moment as it is.

Staying present amidst the holiday hustle doesn't require grand gestures or extra time—it simply involves shifting our perspective and grounding ourselves in the here and now. By incorporating mindful moments into our daily activities, using breathing techniques to regain calm, and embracing gratitude, we can create a holiday experience that is rich with joy and meaning.

Calm Christmas: A Simple Holiday Guide to Mindful Gift Giving, W...

This season, allow yourself to move through each day with mindfulness and presence, savoring the sights, sounds, and connections that make the holidays so special. With these practices, you'll be able to transform holiday stress into holiday joy, experiencing each moment with a peaceful, open heart.

Chapter 8
Mindful Decorations and Ambience

Decorating for the holidays is a way to invite the season's warmth, joy, and spirit into our homes. The colors, lights, scents, and sounds we choose create an atmosphere that shapes how we experience the season. But holiday decorations can sometimes become overwhelming or cluttered, adding to the stress of an already busy time. By approaching holiday decorating with mindfulness, you can create a space that promotes calm, joy, and presence.

This chapter explores how to design a calming holiday environment, use sensory mindfulness to elevate the atmosphere, and embrace simplicity to foster a peaceful, joyful space. Decorating mindfully brings a refreshing sense of intention, helping your holiday space feel like a true sanctuary of warmth and meaning.

Creating a Calming Holiday Space

Holiday decor has the power to set the tone for the entire season, making it essential to choose decorations that inspire calm, comfort, and joy. Instead of aiming to fill every corner with holiday items, consider decorating in a way that promotes a sense of peace and relaxation.

Here are a few ways to create a calming holiday space:

- **Choose a Soothing Color Palette**: Traditional holiday colors are vibrant and festive, but they don't have to be overwhelming. Try using a simplified color palette that feels harmonious and soothing to you. Soft whites, muted greens, golds, and silvers can create a serene winter wonderland effect. If you love brighter colors, consider using them as accents against a neutral background. A calming color scheme makes the space feel less cluttered and more cohesive.
- **Incorporate Natural Elements**: Nature brings an immediate sense of calm and grounding. Adding elements like pine branches, eucalyptus, berries, or pinecones can enhance the holiday spirit while creating a peaceful atmosphere. These natural touches not only look beautiful but also remind us of the simplicity and beauty of nature, helping to balance the season's commercial aspect.

- **Use Lighting to Set the Mood**: Lighting can dramatically affect the ambiance of a room. Soft, warm lighting—whether from candles, fairy lights, or a fireplace—creates a cozy and calming effect. Avoid overly bright lights or flashing bulbs, which can feel chaotic. Instead, opt for steady, warm-toned lights that invite you to relax and linger in the space.
- **Create "Resting Spaces"**: Instead of covering every available surface with decor, leave some "resting spaces" in your home. These are areas with little or no decoration, which allow the eye and mind to rest. This approach prevents overstimulation, making your decorations stand out even more and fostering a balanced, calming environment.

Creating a calming holiday space allows you to fully enjoy the decorations without feeling overwhelmed. By focusing on cohesive colors, natural elements, soothing lighting, and intentional simplicity, you invite a sense of peace and joy into your holiday environment.

The Role of Sensory Mindfulness

Our senses play a huge role in how we experience the holidays, so incorporating sensory mindfulness into your decorations can enhance the atmosphere and create a memorable, joyful space. By thoughtfully engaging sight, smell, touch, and sound, you can build an immersive experience that feels comforting and festive.

Sight: Visual Harmony and Focus

Choose a few focal points in your home, such as the mantel, entryway, or dining table, and decorate them with intention. This allows your eyes to rest on specific, beautiful displays rather than feeling overwhelmed by a visually cluttered space. If you have a tree, consider placing it where it can be easily seen and enjoyed, allowing it to become the heart of your holiday decor. Simplicity and balance in visual elements create an environment that feels both festive and peaceful.

Smell: Holiday Scents and Aromatherapy

Scent is deeply connected to memory and emotion, and holiday scents can evoke a powerful sense of warmth and nostalgia. Try incorporating natural scents like pine, cinnamon, orange, or clove, which can be introduced through essential oils, candles, or dried herbs. Simmering a pot of cinnamon sticks, cloves, and orange slices on the stove can fill your home with a delightful aroma. Keeping scents subtle and natural avoids overstimulation and creates a comforting, inviting atmosphere.

Touch: Textures and Tactile Comfort

Mindfully chosen textures can make a space feel more grounded and cozy. Incorporate soft blankets, plush pillows, and warm fabrics like wool or faux fur. If you have favorite holiday decorations with specific textures, such as felt ornaments, wooden figures, or knitted stockings, bring them into your space. These elements invite touch and add a tactile layer of warmth to the atmosphere, creating a sense of coziness and comfort.

Sound: Calming Holiday Music and Natural Sounds

The right sounds can enhance your holiday space and set a calm, joyful tone. Consider playing soft holiday music or instrumental versions of classic songs to create a relaxing ambiance. You might also enjoy nature-inspired sounds, such as crackling firewood or gentle wind chimes, which can bring a soothing quality to your space. Keeping sounds subtle and gentle contributes to a sense of peace, encouraging you to be present and savor the moment.

Using sensory mindfulness in your holiday decorating engages all the senses, creating a well-rounded, peaceful holiday experience. Each sense adds a layer of meaning and warmth, turning your space into a true sanctuary of holiday joy.

Mindfully Simplifying the Holiday Environment

In a season when more is often seen as better, simplifying your holiday decorations can feel surprisingly liberating. A minimalist approach not only reduces stress but also brings a sense of intentionality and clarity to your space. By embracing simplicity, you allow each decorative element to shine, making your holiday environment feel more meaningful and serene.

Here are a few ways to simplify your holiday decor:

- **Limit Your Color Palette**: Choosing one or two main colors, with perhaps an accent color, creates a cohesive look that feels both elegant and calming. For instance, a combination of green and white with touches of gold can bring a natural, peaceful feel. Limiting colors helps prevent visual clutter and allows you to enjoy each decoration more fully.
- **Curate Your Decorations**: Instead of using all of your holiday decorations, choose a few that hold the most meaning or bring you the most joy. For example, display a treasured set of ornaments on your tree, arrange a few candles on your dining table, or place a simple wreath on your door. Let go of the pressure to

use every item; instead, let each piece you choose to display add intention and beauty to your space.

- **Embrace Space and Balance**: Creating a simplified holiday space doesn't mean it has to feel bare. Use empty spaces and balance as part of your design. For example, a single, well-chosen centerpiece on a table can be more impactful than multiple decorations. Allowing space around each item draws attention to the beauty of each piece and adds a sense of tranquility to the room.
- **Consider Sustainable Decor**: Simplifying can also mean choosing sustainable and eco-friendly decorations. Consider using natural materials, like branches, dried flowers, or twine, and items you can use year after year. Not only does this contribute to a cleaner environment, but it also reinforces the idea that meaningful decorations don't have to be elaborate or commercial. A simple garland of pine branches or a handmade ornament can be just as beautiful as store-bought items.
- **Declutter Before You Decorate**: Before you bring out your holiday decorations, take a moment to tidy and declutter your space. Removing everyday items from shelves or tables creates a blank canvas, making it easier to see where decorations will fit naturally. Decluttering also makes it easier to appreciate each decoration, as there are fewer distractions.

Simplifying your holiday decor is about creating a space that feels peaceful, intentional, and meaningful. With fewer, more intentional pieces, your holiday environment becomes a place where you can truly relax, reflect, and enjoy the season.

. . .

Mindful holiday decorating is a way to create an atmosphere that promotes peace, joy, and presence. By approaching your decor with intention—focusing on calmness, sensory mindfulness, and simplicity—you can transform your space into a sanctuary that enriches the holiday season.

Let each decoration be a reminder to slow down, savor each moment, and appreciate the beauty around you. With a mindful approach to your holiday ambience, your space becomes a source of warmth and joy, filling your heart and home with a sense of calm celebration.

Chapter 9
Giving Yourself the Gift of Rest

The holiday season is full of joy, connection, and excitement—but it can also be a time of hustle and exhaustion. In our eagerness to make the holidays special, we often push ourselves to do more and rest less. Yet rest is one of the most valuable gifts you can give yourself during this busy season. Prioritizing rest not only replenishes your energy but also enables you to approach each moment with a calm, joyful presence. When we allow ourselves to slow down and restore, we become more present, resilient, and able to appreciate the true meaning of the season.

In this chapter, we'll explore the importance of rest and how to incorporate it mindfully into your holiday routine. From creating restorative practices to practicing good sleep hygiene, these small acts of self-care will help you move through the season with a peaceful heart and a rested mind.

Prioritizing Rest in a Busy Season

Rest often falls to the bottom of our priority list during the holidays, with so much to accomplish and so many loved ones to see. But far from being a luxury, rest is essential for our well-being. When we give ourselves permission to rest, we're honoring our needs and taking care of ourselves, which in turn allows us to be more present for others.

Think of rest as an essential ingredient in a joyful holiday season. Just as you set time aside for cooking, decorating, and gatherings, setting aside time for rest is a way to nurture yourself and make the most of the season. Here are some tips for making rest a priority:

- **Set Boundaries with Yourself and Others**: It's easy to say "yes" to every invitation and obligation, but overcommitting can quickly lead to burnout. Practice setting gentle boundaries with yourself and others, allowing yourself to say "no" to activities that feel draining. You'll have more energy and focus for the things that truly matter to you.
- **Reframe Rest as a Gift**: Instead of seeing rest as "wasted time" or something you have to earn, view it as a necessary gift you're giving yourself. Just as you want your loved ones to enjoy the holidays, remember that

you also deserve a joyful, restful season. Giving yourself rest is a way to show kindness and care to yourself.
- **Plan for "Rest Days"**: If your calendar is filling up with holiday events, pencil in dedicated rest days or blocks of time. These can be mini-retreats at home where you allow yourself to relax, read a book, take a bath, or simply do nothing. Even a few hours of intentional rest can make a big difference, helping you recharge and feel ready to enjoy the holiday festivities.

Prioritizing rest isn't about withdrawing from the season—it's about preserving your energy so that you can fully enjoy each moment. By giving yourself the gift of rest, you're investing in a holiday experience that feels balanced, joyful, and meaningful.

Creating a Restorative Holiday Routine

The holiday season brings unique opportunities to establish a restorative routine, one that nurtures both your body and mind. Incorporating small, restorative practices into your days can help you stay grounded, energized, and resilient to stress. By dedicating even a few minutes each day to relaxation, you create a personal oasis of calm that will support you through the season's demands.

Here are some ideas for building a restorative holiday routine:

- **Daily Meditation or Mindfulness Practice**: Set aside a few minutes each day to meditate or simply sit in silence. You could start each morning with a 5-minute breathing exercise, or close the day with a quiet moment of reflection. Mindfulness allows you to center yourself, clear your mind, and approach the day with a sense of calm and clarity. Apps like Headspace

or Calm offer short, guided meditations that can fit easily into a busy schedule.
- **Gentle Yoga or Stretching**: Physical tension often builds up during the holiday season, especially with extra activities like shopping, cooking, and traveling. Incorporating gentle yoga or stretching into your day can help release tension and restore your energy. Try a few simple poses each morning or evening to reconnect with your body and create a moment of peace.
- **Walks in Nature**: Spending time outdoors, even just for a short walk, can have a restorative effect. Nature offers a sense of calm and grounding that's especially beneficial during busy times. If you have access to a park or a quiet outdoor area, take a daily or weekly walk. Notice the sights, sounds, and smells around you, letting yourself connect with the beauty of the season.
- **Journaling and Gratitude**: Writing down your thoughts, reflections, or moments of gratitude can be a restorative way to unwind and reconnect with yourself. Consider keeping a holiday journal where you jot down highlights of each day, reflections, or things you're grateful for. This practice can help you focus on the positives, reduce stress, and bring you closer to the spirit of the season.

Creating a restorative holiday routine doesn't have to be complicated or time-consuming. Even a few minutes of quiet reflection, gentle movement, or fresh air each day can create a foundation of calm that carries you through the season.

. . .

Mindful Sleep Practices

Good sleep is essential for health, well-being, and resilience, yet it's often the first thing sacrificed during busy times. With so many holiday activities and responsibilities, getting a full night's rest can feel like a challenge. Practicing mindful sleep hygiene is a way to ensure that your body and mind get the rest they need, allowing you to wake up feeling refreshed and ready for each day's events.

Here are some mindful sleep practices to help you maintain quality sleep during the holiday season:

- **Create a Consistent Sleep Schedule**: Try to go to bed and wake up at the same time each day, even on weekends or days off. Consistency helps regulate your body's natural sleep-wake cycle, making it easier to fall asleep and wake up feeling rested. If holiday gatherings disrupt your schedule, try to resume it as soon as possible.
- **Establish a Pre-Sleep Routine**: A calming pre-sleep routine signals to your body that it's time to wind down. This might include activities like reading a book, taking a warm bath, dimming the lights, or practicing gentle stretching. Avoid screens and stimulating activities in the hour before bed, as these can interfere with your body's natural transition to sleep.
- **Practice Progressive Relaxation**: Progressive relaxation is a technique that helps release tension in the body, promoting a state of calm and relaxation. As you lie in bed, take a few deep breaths and begin to focus on each part of your body, one at a time. Start with your toes, tensing and then relaxing each muscle group as you move up through your legs, torso, arms,

and face. This practice helps your body fully relax, making it easier to drift into sleep.
- **Limit Caffeine and Sugar in the Evening**: Holiday treats are part of the season's joy, but consuming too much caffeine or sugar in the evening can make it harder to fall asleep. Try to enjoy caffeinated drinks and sweet treats earlier in the day, and switch to herbal teas or water in the evening. A mindful approach to holiday indulgences can help you enjoy the festivities without disrupting your sleep.
- **Create a Calm Sleep Environment**: Your sleep environment plays a big role in the quality of your rest. Make sure your bedroom is cool, quiet, and free from bright lights. Consider using blackout curtains, white noise, or essential oils like lavender to create a relaxing atmosphere that supports restful sleep.

Good sleep hygiene ensures that you're giving your body the rest it needs, helping you wake up each day with a clear mind and a rested body. By approaching sleep mindfully, you set yourself up for a holiday season that feels balanced and energized, allowing you to fully enjoy each day.

In the holiday season, giving yourself the gift of rest is one of the most valuable ways to nurture your well-being. Prioritizing rest, building a restorative routine, and practicing mindful sleep habits help you feel rejuvenated, grounded, and ready to embrace the season with joy.

Let rest be a foundation for your holiday experience, supporting you as you celebrate, connect, and enjoy the beauty of the season. When you make time for rest, you're choosing a holiday filled with presence, peace, and well-being—both for yourself and for those around you.

Creating a Restorative Holiday Routine

The holiday season brings unique opportunities to establish a restorative routine, one that nurtures both your body and mind. Incorporating small, restorative practices into your days can help you stay grounded, energized, and resilient to stress. By dedicating even a few minutes each day to relaxation, you create a personal oasis of calm that will support you through the season's demands.

Here are some ideas for building a restorative holiday routine:

- **Daily Meditation or Mindfulness Practice**: Set aside a few minutes each day to meditate or simply sit in silence. You could start each morning with a 5-minute breathing exercise, or close the day with a quiet moment of reflection. Mindfulness allows you to center yourself, clear your mind, and approach the day with a sense of calm and clarity. Apps like Headspace or Calm offer short, guided meditations that can fit easily into a busy schedule.
- **Gentle Yoga or Stretching**: Physical tension often builds up during the holiday season, especially with extra activities like shopping, cooking, and traveling. Incorporating gentle yoga or stretching into your day can help release tension and restore your energy. Try a few simple poses each morning or evening to reconnect with your body and create a moment of peace.
- **Walks in Nature**: Spending time outdoors, even just for a short walk, can have a restorative effect. Nature offers a sense of calm and grounding that's

especially beneficial during busy times. If you have access to a park or a quiet outdoor area, take a daily or weekly walk. Notice the sights, sounds, and smells around you, letting yourself connect with the beauty of the season.

- **Journaling and Gratitude**: Writing down your thoughts, reflections, or moments of gratitude can be a restorative way to unwind and reconnect with yourself. Consider keeping a holiday journal where you jot down highlights of each day, reflections, or things you're grateful for. This practice can help you focus on the positives, reduce stress, and bring you closer to the spirit of the season.

Creating a restorative holiday routine doesn't have to be complicated or time-consuming. Even a few minutes of quiet reflection, gentle movement, or fresh air each day can create a foundation of calm that carries you through the season.

Mindful Sleep Practices

Good sleep is essential to our health, well-being, and resilience. During busy times like the holiday season, however, sleep is often one of the first things we sacrifice. Between late-night gatherings, extra holiday responsibilities, and the general excitement of the season, getting a full night's rest can become challenging. Yet, quality sleep is one of the best gifts you can give yourself. By practicing mindful sleep hygiene, you ensure that your body and mind get the rest they need, allowing you to greet each day with a refreshed outlook and the energy to fully enjoy each holiday moment.

This chapter introduces mindful sleep practices that can help you maintain quality sleep throughout the holiday season. These small habits are easy to incorporate into your routine and provide a foundation of calm and restfulness that can carry you through even the busiest days.

Create a Consistent Sleep Schedule

Consistency is one of the cornerstones of good sleep. By going to bed and waking up at the same time each day—even on weekends or days off—you help regulate your body's natural sleep-wake cycle, making it easier to fall asleep and wake up feeling rested. While holiday gatherings or activities may disrupt your schedule on occasion, try to return to it as soon as possible.

If you know you'll be out late, consider giving yourself extra rest the next day or scheduling a quiet, restful morning to recover. Consistency creates a rhythm that supports both your energy and mood, allowing you to navigate the holiday season with resilience and presence.

Establish a Pre-Sleep Routine

A pre-sleep routine signals to your body that it's time to wind down and prepare for rest. This can include soothing activities like reading a book, taking a warm bath, dimming the lights, or practicing gentle stretching. The goal is to ease yourself into a calm state, away from the hustle of the day.

Try to avoid screens, like phones or TVs, in the hour before bed. The blue light emitted by screens can interfere with melatonin production, the hormone that regulates sleep. Instead, consider swapping screen time for a more relaxing activity, such as listening to calming music, doing a few minutes of mindful breathing, or journaling about the day. A calming pre-sleep routine is a small but powerful way to end the day with intention, setting the stage for a restful night's sleep.

. . .

Practice Progressive Relaxation

Progressive relaxation is a simple technique that releases tension in the body, making it easier to fully relax and drift into sleep. As you lie in bed, take a few deep breaths, and then focus on each part of your body, one at a time. Begin with your toes, tensing and then releasing each muscle group as you move slowly up through your legs, torso, arms, and finally, your face.

This practice helps you become more aware of physical tension and encourages a state of calm that prepares you for sleep. Progressive relaxation also gives your mind something gentle to focus on, allowing you to shift away from thoughts or concerns that might otherwise keep you awake. By letting your body relax in stages, you'll find it easier to sink into a deep, peaceful sleep.

Limit Caffeine and Sugar in the Evening

Holiday treats and beverages are one of the joys of the season, but they can sometimes interfere with sleep. Consuming caffeine or sugar in the evening can make it harder to fall asleep, leaving you feeling restless and alert when it's time to wind down. To support a good night's sleep, try to enjoy caffeinated drinks and sugary treats earlier in the day, and switch to herbal teas or water in the evening.

For a relaxing nighttime drink, consider caffeine-free options like chamomile tea, peppermint tea, or warm milk, which can help signal to your body that it's time to start winding down. By being mindful of your caffeine and sugar intake, you can enjoy holiday indulgences without disrupting your sleep routine.

Create a Calm Sleep Environment

Your sleep environment plays a significant role in the quality of your rest. By creating a calm, comfortable space, you set yourself up for a night of deep, rejuvenating sleep. Here are a few ways to make your bedroom more conducive to rest:

- **Keep It Cool**: A cool room temperature, ideally between 60–67°F (15–19°C), promotes better sleep. You might find it helpful to keep a window slightly open or use a fan if the room feels too warm.
- **Eliminate Light Sources**: Light can disrupt sleep, so make sure your room is as dark as possible. Use blackout curtains if needed, and consider covering any electronic lights or turning them off.
- **Use White Noise or Earplugs**: If you're sensitive to noise, using a white noise machine or earplugs can help block out distractions and create a soothing background sound that encourages sleep.
- **Incorporate Relaxing Scents**: Essential oils like lavender, chamomile, and cedarwood have calming properties that can enhance sleep quality. You can use an essential oil diffuser or place a few drops on your pillow before bed to enjoy a relaxing scent as you drift off.

By creating a calm, comfortable environment, you encourage deeper, more restful sleep. Small changes to your bedroom setup can make a big diffcrence in how well you rest, leaving you refreshed and energized for the next day.

Good sleep hygiene ensures that you're giving your body the rest it needs during the holiday season. By maintaining a consistent sleep schedule, establishing a calming pre-sleep routine, practicing relaxation techniques, and creating a soothing sleep environment, you build a foundation of quality sleep that supports both your physical and mental well-being.

The gift of restful sleep helps you approach each day with a clear mind, a calm heart, and a resilient spirit. Prioritizing sleep as an essential part of your holiday experience allows you to fully enjoy each moment with presence, joy, and peace. Let rest be a foundation for your holiday season, bringing balance and vitality to everything you do. When you make time for sleep, you're choosing a holiday experience that nourishes both body and soul, giving you the strength to connect, celebrate, and embrace the beauty of the season.

Chapter 10
Closing the Year with Mindfulness

As the year draws to a close, it's natural to reflect on what we've experienced, learned, and achieved. The end of the year is a time for contemplation, a chance to take stock of what we've been through, appreciate the moments of joy and growth, and let go of what no longer serves us. By mindfully closing the year, we honor our journey and make space for new beginnings in the coming months.

This chapter is an invitation to reflect on the past year, set meaningful intentions for the year ahead, and consider how to carry the mindfulness practices we've cultivated during the holiday season into daily life. Through journaling prompts, meditation practices, mindful goal-setting, and the continued practice of presence, this chapter guides you through a mindful end-of-year ritual to close the year with gratitude and look forward with clarity and intention.

Reflecting on the Year Past

Reflection allows us to process our experiences and find meaning in them. Taking time to look back on the past year, with both its challenges and triumphs, helps us gain perspective, appreciate our growth, and cultivate a sense of gratitude. This reflection doesn't have to focus solely on accomplishments or successes. Rather, it's an opportunity to celebrate the small moments, honor the lessons learned, and appreciate how far we've come, even if it wasn't always easy.

To start your reflection, find a quiet space where you can focus and relax. You may wish to light a candle, play soft music, or set up a comfortable place to sit or lie down. Once you feel centered, consider these journaling prompts and meditation practices to guide your end-of-year reflection.

Journaling Prompts for Reflection

Journaling is a powerful way to explore your thoughts, feelings, and memories. These prompts are designed to help you reflect on the highlights and lessons of the past year. Take your time with each question, allowing yourself to write freely without judgment or expectation.

1. **What are some of the highlights or memorable moments from this year?**
2. Recall the moments that brought you joy, whether they were big achievements or small, simple pleasures. Write about what made these moments special and what you're most grateful for.
3. **What challenges did I face, and how did I grow from them?**
4. Reflect on the difficulties you encountered and how you navigated them. Consider what you learned, how you adapted, and how these experiences contributed to your resilience or self-awareness.
5. **What did I learn about myself this year?**
6. Consider the personal insights you gained over the year. Maybe you learned something new about your strengths, values, or boundaries. Reflect on how these insights have shaped who you are today.
7. **Who or what am I most grateful for?**
8. Take a moment to acknowledge the people, experiences, or aspects of your life that brought you gratitude. Consider writing a few words about each one, or simply listing them as a way to honor your appreciation.
9. **What do I want to let go of as the year ends?**
10. Think about any habits, thoughts, or patterns that no longer serve you. Allow yourself to reflect on why it's time to release them and imagine how letting go will create space for new possibilities.

Meditation Practice for Reflection

If you prefer a meditation-based reflection, the following practice can help you explore the year's lessons and experiences with mindfulness.

1. **Begin with a few deep breaths**, allowing your mind to settle and your body to relax. Visualize yourself seated at the close of the year, looking back on the months behind you.
2. **Invite a sense of curiosity** about each month or season of the past year. As memories arise, let yourself observe them without judgment, simply noting the emotions, thoughts, and experiences that come to mind.
3. **Focus on gratitude** for the moments that brought you joy or growth. Take a few breaths to appreciate each memory, allowing gratitude to fill your heart.
4. **Release what you need to let go of**: As you reflect, notice if any thoughts or memories bring a sense of heaviness or tension. Imagine these experiences as leaves on a stream, gently floating away, and allow yourself to let go with each exhale.
5. **Close the meditation with an intention for peace** as you transition into the new year. Hold this intention in your heart, letting it guide your final breaths of the practice.

Reflection creates a sense of closure, helping you feel complete and ready to welcome the year ahead with a grounded, open heart.

Mindful Goal-Setting for the New Year

As a new year begins, many of us feel inspired to set goals or make resolutions. Yet, traditional resolutions often center on strict self-improvement, setting high expectations that can leave us feeling pressured or even overwhelmed. Mindful goal-setting offers a gentler, more fulfilling approach, where goals are grounded in kindness, self-acceptance, and meaningful intention. This practice focuses on aligning with our values, fostering growth, and supporting our well-being, rather than adhering to rigid achievements.

Mindful goals emphasize progress over perfection, intention over results. By setting mindful goals, you embrace a journey rooted in curiosity and self-compassion, allowing you to pursue what truly matters to you in a way that feels inspiring rather than burdensome. In this chapter, we'll explore a framework for mindful goal-setting that encourages you to align with your values, focus on intentions, and make space for flexibility and growth.

1. Focus on Intentions Rather Than Outcomes

One of the key differences between traditional goals and mindful goals is the emphasis on intention over outcome. While traditional resolutions often zero in on specific, measurable achievements, mindful goals focus on the underlying purpose or feeling you wish to cultivate. Setting an intention helps you clarify your values, giving your goals a sense of direction and meaning, rather than a fixed destination.

For example, instead of setting a goal like "exercise five times a week," consider an intention that reflects why movement is important to you, such as "taking time to care for my body through movement." This approach allows for flexibility and adapts to your needs on any given day. If some weeks you only exercise twice or try a new type of movement, you're still honoring your intention and nurturing your well-being.

Intentions also allow for a broader range of expressions. If your intention is "to cultivate calm," there are many ways you can work toward it, from practicing mindfulness to taking nature walks to organizing your space. Intentions give you the freedom to explore different paths toward a meaningful goal, keeping your journey engaging and adaptable.

Intentional Goal-Setting Prompts

To explore your intentions for the new year, try these reflective prompts:

- **What values do I want to honor this year?**
- Reflecting on your values can help you set goals that feel meaningful and aligned with who you are.
- **How do I want to feel each day?**
- This question can help you focus on intentions that enhance your emotional and mental well-being, like cultivating joy, peace, or gratitude.
- **What qualities do I want to develop?**
- Think about the traits or habits you'd like to nurture, such as patience, resilience, or creativity, and consider how you can incorporate them into your goals.

2. Set Realistic and Attainable Goals

Mindful goal-setting is about creating goals that support your well-being, not ones that feel burdensome. It's easy to feel ambitious at the start of a new year, but setting goals that are too large or demanding can lead to burnout. Instead, aim to set goals that are realistic within your current lifestyle and circumstances.

Starting with small, sustainable changes ensures that your goals feel manageable and encourages consistency. For instance, if you want to practice mindfulness, rather than setting a goal to meditate for an hour each day, begin with five or ten minutes.

Gradual, achievable steps make it easier to incorporate new habits into your routine and help you build confidence and momentum.

Consider breaking larger goals into smaller, actionable steps. If your goal is to "spend more time in nature," begin with a weekly walk in a nearby park or a short outdoor break each day. Over time, you may find it natural to increase the frequency or duration of these activities, but starting small allows you to ease into new habits without pressure.

Examples of Realistic Mindful Goals

Here are some ideas for goals that align with a mindful, sustainable approach:

- **Practice gratitude daily** by writing down one thing you're grateful for each day.
- **Add one healthy meal a week** that incorporates more vegetables or whole foods.
- **Dedicate five minutes each morning** to mindful breathing or meditation.
- **Spend one hour each week in nature,** whether it's a walk in a park or simply sitting outside.

Realistic, attainable goals build confidence and consistency, helping you experience positive change without the pressure to do it all at once.

3. Embrace Progress Over Perfection

In any journey, growth is rarely a straight line. Embracing a mindset of progress over perfection allows you to celebrate each step forward, no matter how small, and view setbacks as part of the process. When you set mindful goals, it's natural for progress to ebb and flow. Some weeks may be more productive than others, and unexpected challenges may arise. The key is to remember that each step, no matter the size, is a meaningful part of your journey.

Mindful goal-setting involves practicing self-compassion, especially when things don't go as planned. Instead of feeling discouraged by a missed step or imperfect progress, treat yourself with the same kindness you would offer a friend. Recognize that growth takes time, and every effort contributes to your path forward.

Focusing on progress over perfection encourages a growth mindset. Rather than judging yourself by the final outcome, you can celebrate the small steps, appreciate the journey, and learn from each experience.

Tips for Embracing Progress

- **Acknowledge Small Wins**: Take time to recognize each accomplishment, no matter how minor. Each small step is part of your progress.
- **Practice Self-Compassion**: When things don't go as planned, remind yourself that it's okay. Offer yourself words of kindness and encouragement, remembering that growth takes time.
- **Keep a "Progress Journal"**: Documenting your journey can help you see how far you've come, even if progress feels slow. Reflect on the challenges you've overcome and the ways you've grown.

4. Review and Adjust Regularly

Mindful goals are dynamic; they are flexible and open to change. As life evolves, so do our needs, desires, and priorities, making it essential to periodically review and adjust our goals. This flexibility allows you to adapt your goals based on your current circumstances and prevent feelings of guilt or disappointment if things don't unfold as expected.

Consider setting aside time each month or season to reflect on your goals, evaluate what's working, and adjust as needed. Perhaps a goal that felt important at the beginning of the year no longer resonates, or you find that a new interest or value has emerged. Regular reviews allow your goals to grow with you, ensuring they continue to align with your authentic self.

Monthly Reflection Prompts

These prompts can help guide your regular goal check-ins:

- **What progress have I made toward my goals this month?**
  - Recognize the small steps you've taken and celebrate your efforts.
- **Do these goals still align with my current values and needs?**
  - Reflect on whether your goals feel relevant to your current life.
- **What adjustments would make my goals more supportive or achievable?**
  - Consider any changes that could make your goals feel more manageable or meaningful.

Examples of Mindful Goals

To give you a starting point, here are some examples of mindful goals that prioritize well-being, growth, and presence. These goals can serve as inspiration, but remember to tailor your own goals to reflect your unique values and desires.

1. **Dedicate a few minutes each morning to mindfulness or meditation**
2. Setting aside a few moments each day for meditation can help you start each day with calm and intention.
3. **Spend more time in nature by taking weekly walks**
4. Nature has a restorative effect on the mind and body, making it a valuable goal for relaxation and presence.
5. **Practice gratitude by writing down three things you're grateful for each day**
6. Cultivating gratitude can boost your mood and help you stay focused on the positives in life.
7. **Focus on building a self-compassion practice by speaking kindly to yourself**
8. Self-compassion supports mental and emotional well-being, encouraging resilience and self-acceptance.
9. **Create a weekly routine for connecting with loved ones**
10. Connection with others fosters a sense of community and well-being. Whether it's a phone call, shared meal, or simple message, regular connection nurtures relationships.

Mindful goal-setting invites you to create goals that align with your values, nurture your well-being, and allow you to grow at your own pace. By focusing on intention, setting realistic expectations, celebrating progress, and regularly reviewing your goals, you create a framework that supports sustainable, positive change.

This approach allows you to enter the new year with a sense of curiosity and self-kindness, choosing goals that inspire and uplift rather than pressure. Let these mindful goals be a gentle guide through the coming months, helping you to stay grounded, joyful, and connected to what truly matters.

Conclusion: A Mindful Christmas, A Meaningful Life

The holidays are a time to gather, celebrate, and cherish the beauty of life's simple pleasures. Embracing a mindful, simplified approach to Christmas allows us to savor each moment, focusing on what truly matters rather than getting swept up in the pressures of a busy season. By celebrating simplicity, finding calm in tradition, and honoring our well-being, we create a Christmas that is deeply fulfilling and rooted in presence. And as the holiday season

Conclusion: A Mindful Christmas, A Meaningful Life

comes to a close, the gifts of mindfulness can carry us forward, guiding us through each season and every chapter of life with a greater sense of peace, purpose, and joy.

This conclusion is a reflection on the journey of a mindful Christmas and an invitation to carry these practices into everyday life, creating not just a meaningful holiday season but a life rich in intention, gratitude, and simplicity.

Celebrating Simplicity

A mindful approach to Christmas teaches us to embrace simplicity as a way to find deeper fulfillment. Rather than overextending ourselves with endless tasks and expectations, we focus on what brings true joy and connection. By slowing down, decluttering our spaces and schedules, and centering on the relationships, traditions, and rituals that feel meaningful, we transform the holiday season into a time of genuine peace and gratitude.

The Benefits of a Simplified Holiday

The simplicity we cultivate during the holidays offers many gifts that reach beyond the season:

- **Greater Joy in the Present Moment**: A simplified holiday invites us to savor each experience, whether it's a quiet moment with loved ones, the warmth of a cozy home, or the taste of a favorite holiday treat. We find joy not in the quantity of our celebrations but in their quality, allowing us to enjoy each moment with full presence.
- **Reduced Stress and Anxiety**: By releasing unnecessary obligations and letting go of perfection, we reduce the holiday stress that often comes from

Conclusion: A Mindful Christmas, A Meaningful Life

trying to do too much. Simplifying our traditions, gift-giving, and decorations helps us prioritize peace and well-being over external expectations.

- **Meaningful Connection with Others**: When we're not rushing from one event to the next, we have the time and energy to truly connect with those around us. A simplified holiday season allows us to engage in heartfelt conversations, create new memories, and deepen our relationships.
- **Focus on Values and Intentions**: Simplifying Christmas allows us to focus on the values that matter most to us, such as kindness, gratitude, generosity, and presence. Instead of getting caught up in the commercialism of the season, we align our actions with our beliefs, creating a holiday that reflects who we truly are.

A mindful and simplified approach to Christmas reminds us that joy is found in simplicity, and that the most beautiful moments are often those that are quiet, thoughtful, and intentional.

Carrying Calm Beyond Christmas

While the mindful practices we've explored have enriched the holiday season, they don't have to end with the year. By continuing these habits beyond Christmas, we create a life that is more centered, peaceful, and joyful—one in which mindfulness becomes a guiding principle. Whether it's through moments of gratitude, mindful breathing, or intentional goal-setting, each practice supports us in cultivating a calm, meaningful life.

Conclusion: A Mindful Christmas, A Meaningful Life

Making Mindfulness an Ongoing Practice

Here are a few ways to carry the gifts of mindfulness into the months ahead, allowing the calm you've created to sustain you through life's ups and downs:

- **Start Each Day with Presence**: Begin each morning with a mindful moment, setting an intention for the day or simply taking a few deep breaths. This small act centers you before the day begins, allowing you to approach each moment with awareness.
- **Embrace Simplicity in Daily Life**: Just as simplifying your holiday season brought greater peace, you can continue this practice in your daily life. Clear clutter from your home, prioritize what truly matters, and focus on quality over quantity in your activities and relationships. A life of simplicity is one that leaves space for the experiences that bring you the most joy.
- **Practice Gratitude Regularly**: Cultivating gratitude doesn't need to be limited to special occasions. Make a habit of noticing the small moments that bring you happiness and writing down what you're grateful for each day or week. This practice helps you stay connected to the abundance in your life, fostering a positive mindset even during challenging times.
- **Find Mindful Moments in Everyday Activities**: Just as you practiced mindfulness in holiday traditions, try bringing awareness to your everyday activities. Whether you're cooking, driving, or simply taking a break, allow yourself to focus on the sensations, sights, and sounds around you. These mindful pauses reconnect you to the present, helping you move through each day with calm.

Conclusion: A Mindful Christmas, A Meaningful Life

- **Reflect and Recenter as Needed**: Life is full of changes, and mindfulness allows us to adapt with grace. Take time each month to reflect on your goals, intentions, and well-being, making adjustments as needed. This regular check-in helps you stay aligned with your values and supports you in creating a life that feels balanced and fulfilling.

A Mindful Christmas, A Meaningful Life

The journey toward a mindful Christmas is also a journey toward a more meaningful life. Through simplicity, presence, gratitude, and intention, we create a holiday season that reflects our deepest values and nourishes our well-being. By carrying these practices into each new season, we continue to cultivate a life of peace, connection, and joy.

As you move forward, remember that mindfulness isn't about perfection or doing everything "right." It's a gentle practice of awareness, one that invites you to approach each moment with curiosity, compassion, and acceptance. The calm and joy you find in these moments are gifts that stay with you, enriching your life and supporting you through every experience.

May the simplicity and peace of a mindful Christmas continue to fill your days, guiding you on a journey of meaning and fulfillment. Let this season be a reminder that the most precious gifts are those we carry within ourselves—the gifts of presence, gratitude, and a heart open to the beauty of each moment. Embrace the year ahead with mindfulness and intention, creating a life that is rich in purpose and deeply, beautifully your own.

Carrying Holiday Mindfulness Into Everyday Life

The mindfulness practices you've cultivated during the holiday season don't have to end as the new year begins. Carrying these

Conclusion: A Mindful Christmas, A Meaningful Life

practices into your daily life creates a foundation of peace and presence that supports you year-round. From mindful breathing and gratitude to simplifying routines, these habits can enrich your everyday life, helping you remain grounded even during busy times.

Here are ways to bring holiday mindfulness into the rest of the year:

1. Start Each Day with Intention

Just as you might have started holiday mornings with gratitude or mindfulness, continue this practice into the new year. Take a few moments each morning to set an intention for the day. This could be something simple, like "approaching today with patience" or "focusing on moments of joy." Setting an intention helps you carry mindfulness into your daily actions.

2. Practice Weekly Reflection

Regular reflection keeps you connected to your goals, values, and well-being. At the end of each week, set aside a few minutes to reflect on the past few days. Consider what brought you joy, what challenges arose, and what you're grateful for. This ongoing reflection allows you to adjust your intentions and appreciate your progress over time.

3. Simplify Your Environment

During the holidays, you may have experienced the benefits of simplifying decorations and decluttering. Consider extending this principle into your everyday surroundings. Regularly tidying and organizing your space creates an environment that promotes calm and clarity, allowing you to feel more centered at home.

4. Keep a Gratitude Journal

Gratitude is one of the most powerful practices for cultivating mindfulness and joy. Continuing to write down what you're grateful for—whether daily or weekly—reminds you to appreciate the small, beautiful moments in life. Over time, a gratitude journal

Conclusion: A Mindful Christmas, A Meaningful Life

becomes a collection of memories that bring happiness and perspective.

5. Incorporate Mindful Breathing into Daily Routines

Mindful breathing is a simple yet effective way to reduce stress and anchor yourself in the present. Make it a habit to take a few deep breaths whenever you feel stressed or rushed. You can even integrate mindful breathing into daily routines, such as while commuting, waiting in line, or preparing meals.

6. Schedule Regular Time for Self-Care

Continuing self-care practices like meditation, yoga, or nature walks throughout the year ensures that you maintain balance and well-being. Self-care doesn't have to be time-consuming; it can be as simple as setting aside a few minutes each day to check in with yourself, stretch, or enjoy a moment of quiet.

7. Remember to Pause and Appreciate the Present Moment

One of the most valuable aspects of holiday mindfulness is learning to pause and savor each moment. Carry this habit forward by periodically pausing to appreciate what's around you—the sound of birds, a warm cup of tea, or a kind smile from a stranger. These pauses help you stay connected to the beauty in everyday life.

Carrying holiday mindfulness into the new year creates a foundation of peace, resilience, and gratitude that supports you through life's ups and downs. These simple practices, cultivated consistently, help you stay grounded, find joy in the small moments, and approach each day with presence and purpose.

Closing the year with mindfulness is a gift you give yourself. By reflecting on the past, setting mindful goals for the future, and carrying forward the habits of mindfulness, you create a foundation

Conclusion: A Mindful Christmas, A Meaningful Life

for a life filled with intention, joy, and gratitude. As you move into the new year, let mindfulness be your guide, reminding you to cherish each moment, honor your well-being, and embrace the beauty in both the ordinary and the extraordinary. This mindful transition is not just a way to end the year; it's a way to live well every day, building a life rich with meaning, connection, and peace.

Bonus: 30-Day Mindful Holiday Challenge

The 30-Day Mindful Holiday Challenge is designed to help you approach the holiday season with calm, joy, and intention. Each day includes a simple prompt or exercise that encourages mindfulness, self-reflection, or self-care, creating a peaceful, fulfilling holiday experience. You can follow the challenge day by day, or pick and choose the prompts that resonate most with you. Let this challenge guide you through a season filled with presence, gratitude, and joy.

Bonus: 30-Day Mindful Holiday Challenge

Week 1: Grounding and Setting Intentions

Focus on grounding yourself in the present and setting mindful intentions for the season.

1. **Set an Intention**
2. Reflect on how you want to feel this holiday season. Write down an intention, such as "calm," "gratitude," or "connection," and revisit it throughout the month.
3. **Gratitude Journal**
4. Write down three things you're grateful for today. Keep this list somewhere visible to remind you of the blessings around you.
5. **Mindful Breathing**
6. Take five deep, mindful breaths whenever you feel rushed today. Focus on the sensation of air entering and leaving your body.
7. **Digital Declutter**
8. Spend 10 minutes deleting emails or organizing files. Create a calm digital space as a first step toward simplifying the season.
9. **Set Boundaries**
10. Consider one holiday obligation that feels overwhelming. Practice saying "no" or setting a boundary, focusing on prioritizing your well-being.
11. **Intentional Shopping**
12. Before purchasing a holiday gift, pause and reflect on its meaning. Is it something that truly reflects the recipient's personality or needs?
13. **Create a Cozy Corner**
14. Designate a corner of your home for relaxation. Add a blanket, candle, or favorite book, and commit to spending a few minutes there each day.

Bonus: 30-Day Mindful Holiday Challenge

Week 2: Practicing Presence

This week, focus on mindful awareness and savoring the present moment.

15. **Single-Tasking**
16. Choose one task today—such as wrapping gifts or cooking—and do it without distractions. Focus on each step, bringing your full attention to the process.
17. **Mindful Listening**
18. During a conversation today, practice listening without interrupting or planning your response. Notice how this affects your connection with the other person.
19. **Savor a Meal**
20. Take time to fully enjoy one meal today. Notice the flavors, textures, and smells of your food, savoring each bite without distractions.
21. **Holiday Scent Meditation**
22. Choose a seasonal scent (like pine, cinnamon, or peppermint), close your eyes, and breathe it in mindfully for a minute. Notice the memories or emotions it brings up.
23. **Slow Down Your Steps**
24. As you walk today, slow down and notice the sensations in your feet. This simple practice helps ground you in the present moment.
25. **Connect with Nature**
26. Spend a few minutes outside, whether it's a walk or simply standing in your yard. Take in the sounds, smells, and sights around you.
27. **Mindful Music**

Bonus: 30-Day Mindful Holiday Challenge

28. Listen to a holiday song you love, focusing on each note, instrument, and lyric. Let yourself be fully absorbed in the experience.

Bonus: 30-Day Mindful Holiday Challenge

Week 3: Nurturing Self-Care and Joy

Prioritize self-care and cultivate joy with small, nurturing activities.

29. **Self-Care Check-In**
30. Reflect on one thing you can do today to support your well-being. Whether it's drinking more water, stretching, or taking a nap, commit to doing it.
31. **Write a Holiday Letter to Yourself**
32. Write a letter celebrating your strengths and resilience this year. Save it to read at the end of the month or next holiday season.
33. **Mindful Tea or Coffee Ritual**
34. Prepare a warm drink mindfully. Notice the smell, warmth, and taste with each sip, letting it be a calming ritual in your day.
35. **Embrace Silence**
36. Turn off background noise for 5 minutes, allowing yourself a few moments of silence. Notice the thoughts and sensations that arise.
37. **Let Go of Perfection**
38. Reflect on one holiday task where you're aiming for perfection. Practice letting go of the need for it to be "just right" and embrace the beauty of imperfection.
39. **Write Down a Fun Memory**
40. Think of a favorite holiday memory and write it down in detail. Reliving joyful moments can uplift your mood and spark gratitude.
41. **Take a Mindful Bath or Shower**
42. Use this daily ritual to practice mindfulness. Notice the warmth, the feel of the water, and allow yourself to fully relax and unwind.

Week 4: Reflecting and Setting Intentions for the New Year

Use this final week to reflect on the season and set intentions for the new year.

43. **Reflect on Your Accomplishments**
44. Write down a few accomplishments from the past year, big or small. Take time to appreciate the progress you've made.
45. **Mindful Goal Setting**
46. Set one mindful goal for the new year that aligns with your values and well-being, such as practicing gratitude or spending more time in nature.
47. **Release and Let Go**
48. Reflect on any stress, worry, or expectations that you want to release before the new year. Write them down and, if possible, tear up the paper as a symbol of letting go.
49. **Gift Yourself Rest**
50. Give yourself permission to rest today, even if it's for just 10 minutes. Lie down, close your eyes, and let go of any "to-dos" or holiday stress.
51. **Plan a Nature Outing**
52. Schedule a time to spend in nature during the holiday or new year. It could be a walk, a hike, or even stargazing. Let it be a time for reflection and peace.
53. **Write a Gratitude List for the Year**
54. Reflect on the past year and write a list of things you're grateful for, from relationships to moments of joy. Re-read this list whenever you need a boost of positivity.
55. **Create a Vision Board or Journal Page**

56. Gather images, quotes, or words that resonate with how you want to feel in the coming year. Use this as a visual reminder of your intentions.
57. **Meditate on New Beginnings**
58. Take a few minutes to meditate on the idea of new beginnings. Visualize the upcoming year with openness, curiosity, and self-kindness.
59. **Celebrate the Season Mindfully**
60. Spend time with loved ones or in quiet reflection, celebrating the season with mindfulness. Take a moment to honor your journey through the challenge and the mindful practices you've cultivated.

Bonus: 30-Day Mindful Holiday Challenge

This 30-day challenge is a journey to experiencing a calmer, more joyful holiday season. By practicing small daily acts of mindfulness, self-care, and reflection, you nurture yourself amidst the busyness of the season. These prompts are not only a way to enrich the holidays but also an invitation to carry mindfulness into the new year, cultivating a life filled with presence, gratitude, and peace. Enjoy each mindful moment and let this challenge be a gentle guide through a meaningful, fulfilling holiday season.

About the Author

Clara Joy Morgan is a mindfulness coach, wellness writer, and seasoned holiday enthusiast known for her compassionate approach to living mindfully in all seasons of life. Raised in a small town with family-centered holiday traditions, Clara developed a deep appreciation for simplicity and intentional living from an early age. Her background in psychology and years of experience in mindfulness training have uniquely equipped her to guide readers in finding peace, presence, and joy amid the holiday hustle.

With over a decade of experience in mindfulness and wellness, Clara has led numerous workshops and retreats, helping individuals embrace calm and clarity. Her work has been featured in wellness publications and online magazines, where she shares her insights on reducing stress, fostering meaningful connections, and savoring life's simplest pleasures.

A lifelong lover of the holiday season, Clara combined her expertise in mindfulness with her love for Christmas to create *Calm Christmas: A Simple Holiday Guide to Mindful Gift Giving, Wellness, and Traditions*. Through this book, she inspires readers to embrace a more joyful, grounded holiday experience that celebrates what truly matters.

When she isn't writing or teaching, Clara enjoys crafting homemade gifts, hiking with her family, and savoring a good cup of peppermint tea by the fire. She currently resides in the Pacific

Northwest with her husband, two children, and a golden retriever named Holly.

www.ingramcontent.com/pod-product-compliance
Lightning Source LLC
LaVergne TN
LVHW050028080526
838202LV00070B/6969